MATH
FOR
Grownups

Relearn the Arithmetic You Forgot from School So You Can:

Calculate how much that raise will really amount to (after taxes)

Figure out if that new fridge will actually fit

Help a third grader with his fraction homework

Convert calories into cardio time

WITHDRAWN

LAURA LAING

BS, Math Educator

Aadamsmedia

Avon, Massachusetts

Published by
Adams Media, a division of F+W Media, Inc.
57 Littlefield Street, Avon, MA 02322. U.S.A.
www.adamsmedia.com

ISBN 10: 1-4405-1263-9
ISBN 13: 978-1-4405-1263-6
eISBN 10: 1-4405-2689-3
eISBN 13: 978-1-4405-2689-3

Printed in the United States of America.

10   9   8   7   6   5   4   3   2   1

Library of Congress Cataloging-in-Publication Data
Laing, Laura.
Math for grownups / Laura Laing.
p. cm.
Includes index.
ISBN 978-1-4405-1263-6
1. Mathematics—Popular works. I. Title.
QA93.L27 2011
510—dc22
2011010369

This publication is designed to provide accurate and authoritative information with regard to the subject matter covered. It is sold with the understanding that the publisher is not engaged in rendering legal, accounting, or other professional advice. If legal advice or other expert assistance is required, the services of a competent professional person should be sought.
—From a *Declaration of Principles* jointly adopted by a Committee of the American Bar Association and a Committee of Publishers and Associations

Many of the designations used by manufacturers and sellers to distinguish their product are claimed as trademarks. Where those designations appear in this book and Adams Media was aware of a trademark claim, the designations have been printed with initial capital letters.

This book is available at quantity discounts for bulk purchases.
For information, please call 1-800-289-0963.

Dedication

For my three favorite mathematicians:
Dad, Gina, and Zoe.

Contents

Introduction

Everyday Math: Easier Than Running Out of Paint

The numbers game plays a starring role in almost every part of daily life, from making dinner to planning a weekend getaway. Heck, you need math to order a pizza.

Even people who don't sweat math problems—namely, mathematicians!—sometimes have trouble with the calculations we face in everyday life. So it's no wonder that those of us who have already forgotten what we learned in high school (or, worse, never liked math and didn't do well in it) can sometimes stare at a math problem and not have the faintest idea what to do about it.

But luckily you don't have to be Stephen Hawking (or even be proficient with a scientific calculator) to use math in ordinary situations. Remember, it's only a tool. (And it's not even one that requires safety glasses or special training so you won't cut off the tip of your left index finger.) It's a language that describes how our world fits together. Math enables us to make predictions and quick decisions. Math helps us feel powerful and confident.

Here's the honest truth: Adding fractions is no harder than signing up for the office football pool or buying airline tickets online or remembering how to create a folder on your computer desktop. It may just *seem* more challenging.

The truth is that very few people in the world can't do math. You are not one of them. Here's the thing—most math doesn't require you to remember how to find the slope of a line (or even to remember what slope is). The everyday stuff is a combination of basic arithmetic and your innate understanding of how to speak the language of numbers, shapes, and measurements.

Yep, innate. You were born with curiosity about the world around you. Math is just one way to describe that world. And, like it or not, it's a pretty important way.

So unless you don't care what's in your bank account or whether your new elliptical machine will fit through the door of your exercise room, you're going to have to do some math.

And you might as well think you're good at it, right? (Because, guess what? You are.)

You don't have to know calculus to figure out how to lower your monthly mortgage payments. You don't have to remember the Pythagorean Theorem to lose a few extra pounds. And you don't have to do long division in your head to buy paint for your new house.

You do need to have an open mind and a sense of humor. After all, it's only math.

At the Store: Deal or No Deal?

Unless you just hit the Lotto jackpot, you're probably looking for ways to save a little cash at the register. Whether you're buying groceries or the perfect knickknack for your newly decorated living room, keeping more money in your wallet can be a real challenge. The key is to plan ahead and stay sharp.

Estimation Is Your Friend

What's more important: finding your server's tip to the penny or getting out of the restaurant with your sanity intact? We all know some of those folks who obsessively use a calculator to find the tip on their morning bagel and coffee, but how much fun are they? (And how much fun are they having?)

Estimation is your best friend. Need to split the lunch bill with your best friends? Estimate. Need to know how far apart to plant your begonias? Estimate. Want to know how long it will take you to get to Grandma's house for Thanksgiving dinner? Estimate.

When you estimate, you create math problems that are simple to solve in your head. You round numbers so that they're easy to add, subtract, multiply, or divide. You evaluate what you can do well and apply those strategies to the problem at hand. In short, you look for ways to do mental math.

But you are not guessing. In some instances, you're finding a range of possible solutions that make sense. (What's my ETA?) In other situations, you're merely figuring out the answer to a yes-or-no question. (Can I afford to buy those designer shoes?) And sometimes you just don't need to have the answer down to the penny. (How much can I expect to pay each month for my mortgage?)

Mathematicians and scientists estimate all the time—even when they're looking for an exact answer. Estimating helps you judge your solution, and this in turn can keep you out of embarrassing situations (like arriving at the party way too late) *and* hot water (like paying more than you can afford for your not-so-smart phone).

Enough's Enough

Estimating can really pay off when you're in a hurry. And let's face it, who doesn't want to get out of the grocery store as quickly as possible? The cart's squeaky wheel would drive Buddha to distraction.

It's the day before Thanksgiving, and your mother needs five things from the grocery store: pumpkin pie spice, eggs, mini-marshmallows, a jar of olives, and a can of jellied cranberry sauce. Your head hurts from Great-Uncle Pete's incessant shouting, so you gladly volunteer, grabbing the list and a $20 bill from Mom's purse as you head out the door.

Head pounding, you race through the store, find what you need, and end up on the pharmacy aisle. Hey, do you have enough money left for a $4.69 container of aspirin?

Here's what you have in your cart:

- Pumpkin pie spice: $3.15
- Eggs: $3.17
- Mini-marshmallows: $1.15

- Olives: $4.98
- Cranberry sauce: $1.19

When you were in elementary school, you may have learned to estimate by doing the problem and then rounding. But that kind of defeats the purpose, doesn't it? Instead, try rounding first and *then* doing some quick mental math.

$3.15 → $3
$3.17 → $3
$1.15 → $1
$4.98 → $5
$1.19 → $1
$4.69 → $5 (that's the aspirin)

Now you can add up the rounded numbers, speedy quick, to get $18. That's less than the $20 bill you have shoved in your pocket. But wait, there's more!

If you're shopping in a state that charges a sales tax, $20 may not cover it all. Let's just say that the sales tax is 5%. In a rush, and with a screaming headache, how on earth can you find that calculation quickly—and somewhere near accurately?

Remember how to find 10% of a number in your head? Move the decimal point to the left one space: 10% of $10.00 would then be $1.00; 10% of $18.00 would be $1.80.

If you can do that, you can certainly find 5%. Here's how:

10% of $18.00 is $1.80, right?
And 5% is half of 10%, right?
So half of $1.80 is $0.90.

That means your sales tax will be just about $1, and the $20 in your pocket will cover it all.

Whew. That pounding in your temples will be gone in no time.

Math Myths—And Why You Shouldn't Believe Them

Myth 1: There's Only One Way to Skin a Math Problem

Here's the great news. Our brains are designed to solve problems. We do it all the time.

When your kid swears to you that 30 minutes is plenty of time to shower, finish his homework, clear the dinner table, *and* squeeze in one last video game, your brain says, "No way." And your brain is right, even though you didn't have to sit down and calculate that answer.

But brains are like fingerprints—each one is unique. You may have an uncanny ability with maps, while your husband may not be able to find his way out of a paper bag. Or you may be able to read 600 words a minute but have trouble calculating percents.

The key is to find out how *your* brain solves problems.

Here's a quick test. Without using a pencil and paper or a calculator, quickly solve this problem:

$$56 + 25 = ?$$

Now ask someone else to find the answer, but don't tell her how you did it. Then ask her about her process. It's quite possible that she did it differently than you did.

Here are just three ways to find the answer:

Method 1: $56 + 25 = ?$
$50 + 25 = 75$ and $56 - 50 = 6$
$6 + 75 = 81$
so $56 + 25 = 81$

Method 2: $56+25=?$
$60+25=85$ and $60-56=4$
$85-4=81$
so $56+25=81$

Method 3: $56+25=?$
$50+20=70$ and $6+5=11$
$70+11=81$
so $56+25=81$

There are many more approaches, but notice that not one of them requires you to do this:

$$
\begin{array}{r}
56 \\
+\ 25 \\
\hline
81
\end{array}
$$

If you want to line everything up, add the ones digits, carry the 1, and then add the tens digits, go for it. There's nothing wrong with that process either.

But you should feel free to try something new. You're not being graded, and no one is asking you to show your work.

Myth 2: Memorization Is Math's BFF

So you say you're no good at math because you can't remember what 7 times 8 is? Or you claim there's no way you can reduce your mother's enormous chicken casserole recipe, because you don't remember how many pints there are in a quart of milk?

Here's a little secret: You don't have to have these facts down cold in order to use math.

Sure, your fourth grade teacher drilled those multiplication tables into your head. And your middle school math tests included recalling dozens of conversion facts. But since then, you've packed that space between your ears with lots of other useful information—like how to ask where the bathroom is in Spanish and where ESPN is on your cable lineup.

It's completely understandable if you struggle with some basic math facts. And it's completely unnecessary to dig out the flash cards to review.

Instead, use your smarts to figure out arithmetic facts or formulas that you've forgotten. For example: You probably can remember what 10 times 8 is, and you can use that fact to figure out 9 times 8. (10 times 8 is 80, so subtract 8 from 80 to get 72. Voila! That's 9 times 8.)

See, it's much more important to remember the foundation of the times tables—that 9 times 8 just means 9 groups of 8s—than to remember the facts themselves well into your eighties. (And if you do? That's great too!) When you understand *why* arithmetic works, you can make up for most any math fact that you've forgotten.

Still stumped? Head to the web. You can find out how to do *anything* these days by typing a few search terms into a browser. With a click of the mouse, you can access a variety of conversion tables or calculators to choose from. Or a video showing how to find the area of a triangle. The really cool thing is that these instructions are often provided by regular folks, not mathematicians. So you probably have a good shot at finally understanding them. (No offense, math geeks.)

Myth 3: Using a Calculator Is Cheating

Your elementary teacher didn't let you use a calculator to find 6 times 7—and for good reason. She wanted you to learn that fact by heart.

But she's not around anymore.

You wouldn't expect a plumber to fix your pipes without a wrench. And you shouldn't expect to do all math computations with paper and pencil—or in your head. There's no shame in turning to some really great tools to solve your everyday math conundrums. And a calculator is one of them.

The math you do as an grownup is very, very different from what you did as a kid. In math class, you were learning basic ideas, which often meant putting calculators and computers aside. Through that process, you came to understand the foundation of mathematics—how the times tables worked or why adding a negative number is the same as subtracting a positive number.

And now that you have those fundamental concepts humming along with every other idea you use on a daily basis—like language and basic geography—you should feel free to use whatever tools you have at your disposal, whether it's a cheap desktop calculator or your sister, who has that spooky talent for multiplying three-digit numbers in her head.

Look, there are going to be times when you need to do some mental math (figuring out whether a "Big Sale!" means you really can afford that new jacket) or scribble some calculations on a piece of paper (cutting a recipe in half). But if you want to use a calculator, go right ahead. If you need to call your dad for math help, have at it.

Going Mental with Percents

A few percents are really easy to calculate in your head, once you know some shortcuts. (If you don't believe these, check them with a calculator.)

1. 'To take 10% of a number, just move the decimal point one place to the left.

10% of 57.25

5.725

2. To take 5% of a number, find 10% and then take half.

5% of 38

Note that if the decimal point isn't shown, you can just add it to the far right of the number: 38.0 (This zero doesn't change the value of the number at all.)

10% of 38 is 3.8

5% of 38 is 1.9

3. To find 15% of a number—a really handy trick when you're out to dinner and need to calculate a tip—add 10% and 5% of that number. (To make it über-easy, find 10% first.)

15% of 70

10% of 70 is 7

5% of 7 is 3.5

7 + 3.5 = 10.5

4. To find 20% of a number—for when the service is *really* good—just double 10% (that is, multiply it by 2).

20% of 55
10% of 55 is 5.5
5.5 • 2 = 11

(A quick note about that dot between the 5.5 and 2. You probably learned that multiplication is shown with a symbol that resembles a little x, right? So why aren't we showing 5.5 × 2? That works in elementary school, because you haven't done algebra yet. But when you get to middle school and high school, you start using variables—most famously x—to stand for unknown quantities. To avoid confusion between the × that indicates multiplication and the x that represents an unknown quantity, your textbooks probably used a dot, like •, instead of ×. And that's exactly what you'll see in this book, too.)

5. To estimate 25% of a number, round the number to one that is easily divisible by 4 and then divide by 4.

25% of 37
25% of 36
36 ÷ 4 = 9

6. To estimate 50% of a number, round the number to an even number and divide in half (that is, divide by 2).

50% of 69.99
50% of 70
70 ÷ 2 = 35

Decimal Division

Division can be one of the most challenging operations to do in your head. But if you know the multiplication tables, simple problems like $25 \div 2$ shouldn't be too much of a challenge.

A decimal point can throw a wrench in the works, however.

Never fear! Remembering one little rule makes some of these problems child's play.

When you divide a decimal by a whole number (such as 4, 17, or 352), ignore the decimal point—at first. Divide as you would normally do. When you get your answer, look at the number you divided into. Where is the decimal point? In your answer, you want it to be in the same place.

Confused? Here's an example:

You and your colleagues are splitting a box of donuts. The donuts are $3.20, and there are 4 of you. How much does each person owe?

$$\$3.20 \div 4$$
$$320 \div 4 = 80 \text{ (ignore the decimal point at first)}$$
$$\text{so } \$3.20 \div 4 = \$0.80 \text{ (put the decimal point}$$
$$\text{back in where it originally was)}$$

Or how about this one? The grocery store has oranges at 5 for $1.25. You only want one. How much is it going to cost?

$$\$1.25 \div 5$$
$$125 \div 5 = 25$$
$$\text{so } \$1.25 \div 5 = \$0.25$$

It may take a little practice before this process comes easily. But give your gray matter a chance: Next time you're faced with a simple division problem like these, think a moment before you reach for the calculator.

Come Sale Away

Quick! What's 20% of $50? If this question sounds like someone shouting at you in a foreign language, don't panic! You can learn some easy ways to find percents, even if you've already lost the tip chart that came with your new wallet.

But why should you? Well, quickly tabulating percents can help you safely navigate the sales rack at your local department store. Or figure state sales tax while you're on vacation. Or even give your server a decent tip. (Not to mention the warm sensation you have when you know you're being clever.)

In other words, finding percents can help you make smart (and quick) spending decisions—and keep you in the good graces of the barista who knows you prefer decaf instead of high-test coffee every morning.

Let's say you've been dying to get your hands on the newest gourmet ice cream machine. It's listed at $499.99, but you've only saved up $215. Your sister just texted you with great news—in today's paper, she saw an ad announcing a 40% off sale at Chilly Charlie's, your local gourmet ice cream machine store.

Sweet!

You're in your car, just around the corner from Chilly Charlie's, and it would take only a minute to stop in. But is it worth it? Can you afford the purchase?

Three Ways to Estimate

There are a couple of ways to find out—and you won't need paper and pencil, let alone a calculator. (Keep both hands on the wheel!)

First, let's look at what you know:

> **The original price tag on the ice cream maker is $499.99.**
> **It's on sale for 40% off.**
> **You can spend $215.**

The price of the ice cream machine is pretty darned close to $500, so to make things easier, why not do the calculations on $500, instead of $499.99?

Now you have some choices. Try thinking of 40% in a variety of different ways.

- 40% is close to 50%

It's pretty easy to find 50% of $500. Because 50% is the same as half, all you need to do is divide 500 by 2. So 50% of $500 is $250.

That's more than $215—the amount you socked away for that ice cream maker. Will 40% off also be more than you've saved?

Unfortunately, yes.

> **50% of the original price is $250**
> *and*
> **40% off the original price is *less than* 50% off.**
> ***Therefore*,**
> ***40% off* the original price is *more than* $250.**

You still don't have enough money.

Did you see what happened here? You don't necessarily need to find the *exact* sale price. You only need to know whether you can afford to buy the ice cream maker.

- 40% is a multiple of 10%

How Much Is That Zero Worth?

When you're estimating, zeros are a big, big deal. Remembering how to manipulate numbers with zeros is really helpful—and (thankfully) really simple.

Rule: Thou shalt add zeros when multiplying by multiples of 10, 100, 1,000, and so on.

Suppose you have this problem:

$$4,000 \bullet 80,000$$

To get the answer, find $4 \bullet 8$, and then add the zeros on the end. How many zeros, you ask? Why, as many as there are in the original problem!

$$4,000 \bullet 80,000$$
$$320,000,000 \text{ (there are 7 zeros in all)}$$

Rule: Thou shalt drop zeros when dividing by multiples of 10, 100, 1,000, etc.

When you divide with huge numbers that have lots of zeros, just do the opposite of when you multiply—that is, subtract zeros instead of adding them.

$$120,000 \div 6,000$$

Find $12 \div 6$, and then add zeros on the end. How many? Subtract the number of zeros in the second number (the number you're dividing by) from the number of zeros in the first number (the number you're dividing into). That's how many zeros will be in your answer.

$$12 \div 6 = 2$$
$$120,000 \div 6,000 \text{ (subtract 3 from 4 to get 1 zero)}$$
$$20$$

You probably can find 10% of $500 easily, too. In fact, all you need to do is drop the second zero:

$$10\% \text{ of } \$500 = \$50$$

What is 40% of $500?

There are 4 tens in 40 $(4 \bullet 10 = 40)$
and
10% of $500 is $50
so
$4 \bullet \$50 = \$200$

It's tempting to think that the sale price of the ice cream maker is $200, but that mistake could be a costly one. Instead, $200 is the amount you'd *save* if you bought the machine. To find the sale price, you need to do one more step:

$$\$500 - \$200 = \$300$$

Just as we found from the first estimation, the sale price is more than you've saved.

- 40% *off* is 60% *of* the original price

When you take 40% off, you're left with 60% of the original price. That's because

$$40\% + 60\% = 100\%$$

Or, if you prefer subtraction,

$$100\% - 40\% = 60\%$$

Thus, to estimate the sale price of the ice cream maker in one fell swoop, you can use 60% instead of 40%.

Like 40%, 60% is a multiple of 10%.

There are 6 tens in 60 (6 • 10 = 60)
and
10% of \$500 is \$50
so
6 • \$50 = \$300

The sale price is still \$300. And sadly, you still don't have enough saved up.

You may have thought of other ways to look at 40%. Any of these may help you estimate 40% of \$500 without a whole lot of effort. You just need to pick the option that makes most sense to you.

(Go ease your disappointment with a giant banana split.)

Close Enough

Estimation is one of those nifty skills that can help free up your brain for the important stuff—like remembering your debit card PIN or where you parked your car. When you estimate, you don't get bogged down in unnecessary details.

Try these estimation tips:

1. Remember, "good enough" is good enough. You're not trying to get the exact answer, so tell your sense of perfectionism to take five.
2. There is no one right way to estimate.
3. Take the path of least resistance—look for patterns in numbers and operations that make sense to you.
4. Concentrate on the first digits of each number. Rounding to those digits will have the most impact.

5. Look for uncomplicated multiplication and division. Consider rounding to numbers that are easily divisible by 2, 5, or 10.

6. Go for as many zeros as you can. It's easier to multiply 800 by 100 than to multiply 750 by 125.

A Percent Is a Fraction Is a Decimal

From the time you get up in the morning until your head hits the pillow at night, you run into percents dozens of times. The too-cheerful weather guy says there's a 60% chance of rain. (There goes your golf game.) Your cereal has 80% of the recommended daily allowance of fiber. (Yum!) You take home 70% of your gross income. (Thanks, Uncle Sam.) Your boyfriend's cat shredded your new 100% silk pajamas, which you got at a 70% off sale. (He is so out of here!)

But did you remember that percents can be written as fractions or decimals?

If you think about the word *percent*, that makes perfect sense. (Unless you're still preoccupied with your newly destroyed silk PJs.) *Per* means "each." *Cent* means "hundred." So *percent* means "each hundred" or "out of 100." An example will probably help jog your memory.

37% is the same thing as 37 out of 100, which can be shown as $\dfrac{37}{100}$

37 out of 100, or $\dfrac{37}{100}$, is the same thing as 0.37.

Or, in mathematical terms,

$$37\% = \frac{37}{100} = 0.37$$

Conversion Review

Converting percents to fractions or decimals can be really helpful—and really easy.

Convert 25% to a fraction:

Remember, *percent* means "out of 100," so 25% is 25 out of 100, or $\frac{25}{100}$.

But now you need to simplify. What is the biggest number that will divide evenly into both 25 and 100? Divide the top and bottom numbers of the fraction by that number like this: $\frac{25 \div 25}{100 \div 25} = \frac{1}{4}$

Thus 25% is the same thing as $\frac{1}{4}$. (But you probably already knew that.)

Convert 25% to a decimal:

When you convert percents to decimals, you're actually dividing the percent by 100.

$$25\% = 25 \div 100 = 0.25$$

But there's a pattern here that makes things a lot easier. All you are doing is moving the decimal point two places to the left. (Check it with your calculator, if you're suspicious.)

$$25\% \rightarrow 0.25$$

There's no decimal point in 25%, you say? Actually, there is. All numbers have decimal points; if you don't see them, it's just because they've been dropped, and you can put them in at the far right of the number. So the decimal point in 25% is on the right side of the 5, for 25.00. Move it two spaces to the left to produce 0.25.

Clipping Costs

In the late 1800s, C. W. Post began giving out tickets for 1¢ off the price of his new breakfast cereal, Grape Nuts. Who knew that this idea would translate into billions of dollars in savings?

A penny here and a penny there can add up, but using coupons takes some dedication and time. And then there's the question on every shopper's mind: Is it worth it? A few quick calculations can help you find out. Here's an example:

While reading through the Sunday newspaper, Georgia clipped a pile of coupons for her next trip to the local Piggly Wiggly. She also took a few moments to categorize them, and this is what she has:

Paper products	$1.00	50¢	25¢	75¢
Personal hygiene products	$1.50	75¢	50¢	
Pantry items	75¢	75¢	25¢	25¢
Frozen food	25¢	25¢	50¢	
Dairy	50¢			

What's the easiest way for her to figure out how much she'll be saving?

Using an estimation skill will probably help. If she groups like numbers, she can find out her savings in the time it takes to clip a coupon.

$$1 \cdot \$1.50 = \$1.50$$
$$1 \cdot \$1.00 = \$1.00$$
$$4 \cdot 75¢ = \$3.00$$
$$4 \cdot 50¢ = \$2.00$$
$$5 \cdot 25¢ = \$1.25$$

Georgia can now add all of the dollar values to get $8 and all of the change to get 75¢. Her total savings will be $8.75. And on double-coupon day, she'll have, well, doubled her savings to $17.50!

So, is this really a big deal? A little more arithmetic can answer that question. If Georgia shops on double-coupon day each week and averages $8.75 in coupons a week (doubled to $17.50), she'll save $910 each year.

But there are times when using a coupon isn't worth it. That's when you need to "comparison shop."

Georgia has a coupon for 25¢ off the price of That's Italian! Italian salad dressing in the 14-ounce bottle. But her grocery store is advertising a sale on Little Italy Italian dressing. Each 14-ounce bottle is 10% off the regular price. If That's Italian! is $3.95 per bottle and Little Italy is $4.10 per bottle before the sale, which is the better deal: the coupon or the sale?

To find out, Georgia needs to find 10% of $4.10, and subtract that from $4.10 to find the sale price of the Little Italy dressing.

$$10\% \text{ of } \$4.10 \text{ is } 41¢$$
$$\$4.10 - \$0.41 = \$3.69$$

But how much will Georgia save if she uses the coupon to buy That's Italian! dressing?

$$\$3.95 - \$0.25 = \$3.70$$

In fact, she'll save an extra penny by skipping the coupon and buying the dressing that's on sale.

What about on double-coupon day? In that case, it makes more sense to use the coupon:

$$25¢ \cdot 2 = 50¢$$
$$\$3.95 - \$0.50 = \$3.45$$

Now that's a deal!

CHAPTER 1

Let's Make a Deal

It's not like food manufacturers are out to trick you, but they don't necessarily make it easy to figure out the best deal.

Comparison shopping would be much easier if all of the cereal boxes were the same size. Instead, cereals come a variety of different weights—from 12 ounces to 24 ounces. And that doesn't count the bulk packages!

To find the best deal, you'll have to calculate the price per ounce.

(Before you go any further, read the last sentence again. Did a particular word jump out at you? *Per* means "each," as you relearned a few pages ago. And because of that, *per* should also make you think of division. Tuck that idea away for this next example.)

Every day, Jerry enjoys a big bowl of cereal for breakfast, lunch, and dinner. But his new Great Dane is putting a serious cramp in his dining habits. Now Jerry spends his hard-earned cash on the dog, which means he has to cut down on his cereal budget.

How can Jerry still feed his cereal habit, while saving money? Comparison shopping, of course. If he knows which cereals are the best buy, he can keep himself *and* Rufus happy.

The corner supermarket has three brands of corn flakes on the shelf: Kentucky's Best, 'Ears to Health! and Flakes O' Corn. Each brand is a different size, and none of them have the same price:

Kentucky's Best	12 ounces	$3.59
'Ears to Health!	11 ounces	$2.99
Flakes O' Corn	17 ounces	$5.43

If Jerry considers the price per ounce, he can figure out the best deal. To do that, he should divide each box's price by the number of ounces the box contains. (The word *per* was Jerry's big clue that division is involved.)

Let's start with Kentucky's Best, which costs $3.59 for 12 ounces. If we divide $3.59 ÷ 12, we come up with $0.29916 (going on forever). Rounding up, we have a price of 30¢ per ounce. Here's what happens when you do that for each cereal:

Kentucky's Best $3.59 ÷ 12 = 30¢ per ounce
'Ears to Health! $2.99 ÷ 11 = 27¢ per ounce
Flakes O'Corn $5.43 ÷ 17 = 32¢ per ounce

Even though 'Ears to Health! is in the smallest box, it offers the lowest price per ounce.

Drop by Drop

One of America's most expensive habits is drinking bottled water. If the average price of bottled water is $1 per 20 ounces, and you drink about 64 ounces of water every day, you're spending about $3 per day on water. That's $1,095 per year.

Still, drinking tap water may not be an option. In that case, consider a water-filtering system. A pitcher filtering system has a price tag of about $20, and each filter costs about $10. If you need to change the filter after every 40 gallons of water, how much water will you drink before you need to spring for a new filter? There are 128 fluid ounces in a gallon, so multiply to find out: 40 • 128. That's 5,120 ounces. And if you drink 64 ounces of water a day, you can divide to find out that this is 80 days' worth of water (5,120 ÷ 64 = 80).

So the filter costs 12.5¢ per day, or $45.63 per year. Add in the cost of the pitcher, and you're shelling out a whopping $65.63 each year for filtering your own water.

This is $1,029.37 less than you'd spend on bottled water. (Filtering your own water is nicer to Mother Nature, too.)

Buying in Bulk

You've heard this axiom before: Bigger is not always better. And that goes for buying in bulk, too.

Here's an example:

At Miller's Market, the 114-ounce bottle of catsup is $11.98. The 32-ounce bottle is $3.29. Which is the better deal?

Let's calculate:

$11.98 ÷ 114 ounces = 10.5¢ per ounce

$3.29 ÷ 32 ounces = 10.3¢ per ounce

The larger container is actually more expensive than the smaller one.

Why Units Matter

Remember all those times that your math teacher hounded you about putting the units in your answers? Raise your hand if you got a test question wrong because you wrote "14" instead of "14 *pounds*."

Sure, your teacher may have been getting her jollies by insisting that the units matter. (Can't you just hear her maniacal laughter?) But in the real world, if you're not paying attention to your units, you could make a costly mistake.

Let's say you want to compare the powdered lemonade with the stuff premade in the bottle. The powdered drink is measured in grams, but the liquid is measured in ounces. You need to compare like units (grams and grams or ounces and ounces), so what you really need to know is this: How many ounces does the powdered drink make?

Even if the items are packaged in the same units, you may need to be careful.

Take orange juice, for example. You can buy it as a concentrate or already mixed up and ready to go. The units represent different things, though. That's because you're probably not going to drink the concentrate without adding water. You'll get a much more accurate comparison if you consider how much juice the juice concentrate makes.

Here's how that works: Let's say that the can of juice concentrate contains 12 ounces. If the directions say to add 3 cans of water to the juice concentrate, you're adding 12 ounces • 3 or 36 ounces of water. But there's one more thing to consider: You already have 12 ounces of concentrate. So when you mix the juice, you'll end up with 12 ounces + 36 ounces or 48 ounces of juice. And that's what you should use to find your price per unit.

This means you may need to look a little closer at the product label—to avoid comparing lemonade to lemons.

Warehouse Shopping: Whoa! or Woe?

In your dreams, it's the perfect match. You want to save big bucks on groceries, diapers, electronics, even a pretty fountain for the backyard. Your friendly warehouse club offers bulk packaging and, they say, rock-bottom prices.

All you have to do is fork over $50 for an annual membership and figure out where to store those 144 rolls of toilet paper.

But is warehouse shopping a good deal? The truthful answer is yes—and no. Buying in bulk won't necessarily save you a dime. Let's look.

Anabel is considering joining a warehouse club. She's sick and tired of going to the grocery store once a week. Besides, with her husband's compulsion to add to his DVD collection, they could save big on movies. And who knows, maybe she can pick out a nice piece of jewelry for him to give her for Valentine's Day. Would joining the club be a good idea?

She's able to check out the prices online, so she makes up a quick list of items that she buys regularly. She works out the per-unit price, just so she can compare apples to apples (so to speak).

Freezer storage bags at the warehouse store are $33.88 per 250 bags, at a price per bag of 14¢. At the local store, they cost $3.49 for 30 bags, at a price per bag of 12¢. Continuing in this way, Anabel assembles the following information:

Item	Warehouse Cost	Local Store Cost
Storage bags	14¢ per bag	12¢ per bag
Ground coffee	37¢ per ounce	33¢ per ounce
Chicken soup	6¢ per ounce	12¢ per ounce
Soy milk	4¢ per ounce	6¢ per ounce
Bread	8¢ per ounce	12¢ per ounce

At the warehouse club, she'd come out on top buying soup, soy milk, and bread. But the coffee and freezer bags are less expensive at her regular grocery store. Judging on the basis of this list, how much would she be saving at the warehouse store?

First, Anabel adds up the prices per unit at the warehouse store. Then she does the same for the grocery store. Finally, she subtracts to find the savings.

$$14¢ + 37¢ + 6¢ + 4¢ + 8¢ = 69¢ \text{ (warehouse store)}$$
$$12¢ + 33¢ + 12¢ + 6¢ + 12¢ = 75¢ \text{ (local store)}$$
$$75¢ - 69¢ = 6¢ \text{ (difference between local store}$$
$$\text{cost and warehouse store cost)}$$

On these items, using the price per unit, she'll save 6¢.

It might be helpful to think of this in terms of a percent savings, but how does she figure that out? Consider this: Anabel is saving 6¢ for every 75¢ she would have spent at the grocery store. In other words, she's saving 6¢ per 75¢, right? And what does *per* mean? Divide.

$$6¢ \div 75¢ = 0.08, \text{ or } 8\%$$

Based on these items only, Anabel can realize an 8% savings. If she can generalize that savings to her entire grocery list, how much can she save over a year?

Anabel knows she spends about $7,800 each year on groceries, so she takes 8% of $7,800. (But first she needs to convert the percent to a decimal.)

$$8\% \text{ of } \$7,800$$
$$0.08 \cdot 7,800$$
$$\$624$$

$624 a year is not chump change.

There's more to consider, of course. Anabel and her hubby are in the market for some big-ticket items. Accordingly, she makes another list and does the research.

Item	Warehouse	Local Store
Treadmill	$499	$899
Vacuum	$195.52	$241.52
Laptop	$599	$630

Turns out that she can save on all of these items—sometimes a lot! But how much? As before, Anabel adds up the prices of the items and then subtracts to find out:

$$\$499 \text{ (treadmill)} + \$195.52 \text{ (vacuum)} + \$599 \text{ (laptop)} = \$1,293.52$$
$$\$899 + \$241.52 + \$630 = \$1,770.52$$
$$\$1,770.52 - \$1,293.52 = \$477$$

Holy tightwad! She can stash a cool $477 by buying these items at the warehouse club. Added to the $624 she could save each year on her weekly shopping, Anabel can put away $1,101 just by shopping at the warehouse store.

But Anabel also has a $50 membership fee. When she subtracts that cost from her savings, she gets $1,051. The warehouse is still a great deal.

Just don't tell her hubby. He might think they should celebrate with some new DVDs.

Forecasting Frugality

Predicting what you can save over the next year is a bit like developing a weather report. You might have some good models and some past data to base your forecast on, but in the end, just about anything can happen.

So if you're looking for a sure thing, look elsewhere.

Let's say you've estimated that you will save $300 a year by brewing your morning cup of joe instead of buying it on the way to work. But so many things can affect those savings. If you have to replace your $200 coffee maker, you've seriously eaten into your surplus. And if the coffee shop introduces a club card that can save you big bucks, you might just be better off stopping there in the A.M.

And then there is the value of your time. You can calculate this using your hourly salary, or you can use your own logic. Does it take you 3 hours a week to save $15 clipping coupons and researching grocery sales? If your hourly salary is $35, the savings may not be worth it.

Then again, they may be.

If the premium ice cream tastes better than the store brand—and you can afford the difference—buy the premium. If you have a coupon for a large pizza, but you only need a medium, there's no rule that says you can't buy the medium at full price.

Math can be flexible and useful. But it won't tell you what you *must* do. That's because math is both a tool and a language. It facilitates a process and explains why something works.

So calculate your little butt off. Just remember that *you*—not the numbers on the page—make the final decisions.

2

At the Dealership: Leasing vs. Buying, New vs. Used— You Do the Math

Is that cloud of black smoke from your exhaust pipe starting to gag pedestrians? Are you tired of borrowing your brother's beat-up truck to haul your yard-sale treasures home? Did you take an office job, after working from your living room couch for years, and now you have a commute to deal with?

You might just have to visit your friendly car dealership for a new set of wheels.

If the mere mention of this causes heart palpitations, you're not alone. Dealers have a bad reputation for tricking buyers into getting behind the wheel of a vehicle they can't afford. And whether or not this stereotype is true, understanding car-buying math will make you feel more confident about driving a new *or* used car off the lot.

All the Extras

Think the sticker price is what you'll pay for a new vehicle? Think again. You might be able to negotiate a better deal, but even then, you'll probably have a few additional costs to take into account.

Leather seats, a built-in GPS, or top-of-the-line treads may jack up the cost. These are called options, and they're seldom included in the sticker price of the car.

Then there's the destination fee. This may seem like a bogus charge, but it's actually legit. When a dealership orders a new car from the automaker, it doesn't suddenly appear on the lot by some kind of Harry Potter magic. Nope, the automaker must get your new car from their factory to the dealership—without putting any miles on it. Dealerships pass that cost on to you, generally to the tune of a few hundred dollars.

Even if you're shopping at Uncle Alvin's Used Car Extravaganza, there's another thing to consider. Unless you live in Alaska, Delaware, Montana, New Hampshire, or Oregon, you'll need to pay sales tax.

Sales tax is calculated as a percent of the price of the item. And when you purchase a car, it's not like you're picking up a magazine at the airport. The bigger the cost of the item being taxed, the higher the taxes you'll pay. That's why sales tax is a figure worth knowing before you sign on the dotted line.

And there's one more thing to keep in mind: the title and licensing fee. The title proves that you own the vehicle. Paying the licensing fee gives you permission to drive it on public roads. These fees are imposed by the state, so there's no getting around them. And a dealer will usually pass them on to you.

There's no way to predict the title and licensing fee exactly, but you can bet that it'll be between 1% and 1.5% of the cost of the vehicle. The good news (such as it is) is that you don't need to pay taxes on this fee.

How does this all work together? Meet Bubba.

Bubba is ready to go off-road riding, but he has one problem—no truck. So he and his brother Larry are cruising the lot at Nevada Ned's Monster Trucks, looking for a good deal on a great vehicle.

That's where Bubba spies the most gorgeous four-wheel-drive pickup on the planet: fire engine red, an extended cab for his dog, Lady Bird, and a navigation system (so there's no repeat of that bad scene with Larry and Lady Bird last year in the Nevada desert).

The base price is $38,020, without the navigation system. Here are the options:

Luxury package	$1,950
Navigation system	$2,430
Back-up camera	$450
Trailer brake controller	$230
6.2-liter, V-8 engine	$3,000
Moon roof	$995

The sticker also lists an $875 destination charge.

Bubba decides he'd like the navigation system and the bigger engine, but none of the other options. Because he's buying the truck in Nevada, he'll pay a sales tax equal to 6.85% of the purchase price. What's the total price of the truck he wants to buy?

First, Bubba needs to find out how much the options will cost. For the options he wants, he'll spend:

$$\$2,430 + \$3,000 = \$5,430$$

Now he needs to add the cost of the options to the base price of the truck, plus the destination charge:

$$\$38,020 + \$5,430 + \$875 = \$44,325$$

That's when Larry reminds him about the state sales tax, so Bubba whips out his calculator watch once more. Remember how we converted percents to decimals in Chapter 1? In this case, the 6.85% sales tax converts to 0.0685, making it easy to multiply. (At least, it's easy as long as you've got a watch calculator handy. Otherwise, you may have to break out the pencil and paper.)

$$\$44,325 \cdot 0.0685 = \$3,036.26$$
$$\$44,325 + \$3,036.26 = \$47,361.26$$

But wait—there's more. Bubba can't drive his new baby off the lot without a title and license. He's going to have to pay a title and licensing fee, which is probably between 1% and 1.5% of the cost of the truck (without the sales tax). To be on the safe side, Larry recommends finding 1.5% of $44,325.

$$0.015 \cdot \$44,325 = \$664.875$$

Thus Bubba can expect to pay $664.88 for the title and licensing fee. All he has to do now is add that amount to the total he found earlier:

$$\$47,361.26 + \$664.88 = \$48,026.14$$

Now that's a monster price for a monster truck.

Here a Fee, There a Fee

The destination fee may not be negotiable, but other fees are. And some of these are downright phony.

- With the *documentation fee*, the dealer is trying to recoup the cost of drawing up the title, registration, and license.

- *Market adjustments* are fees added to hard-to-get vehicles.
- Don't be fooled by the *transportation fee.* It's not the same as a destination charge, but it is sometimes added if the dealer had to have a specific vehicle delivered for you, from another dealership.
- *Dealer prep* is the cost of preparing the vehicle for delivery.
- *Dealer additions* are becoming rare, but they may include fabric protector and undercoating.
- Finance fees are difficult to spot. To avoid them, arrange your financing before you walk onto the lot.
- Experts advise questioning all *processing and miscellaneous fees.* Buzzwords to look for include *surcharge, assessment, commission, honorarium, recompense, toll,* and *interest.*

One Step, Two Step

After adding on the cost of the options and the destination fee, Bubba found the total cost of the truck by using a two-step process: He found the sales tax and then added it to the price of the truck.

Is there an easier way? Sure!

If you can add 6.85 to 100 in your head, you can find the total price in one fell swoop. That's because the total cost of Bubba's dream truck is 106.85% of $44,325.

$$1.0685 \cdot \$44,325 = \$47,361.26$$

Why does this work? The answer comes from elementary arithmetic, my friend. First, let's compare the two methods. Method 1 is to multiply the cost of the truck by the sales tax rate and then add the answer to the cost of the truck.

$$(\$44,325 \cdot 0.0685) + \$44,325$$
$$\$3,036.26 + \$44,325$$
$$\$47,361.26$$

Now see what happens when you add 1 to the sales tax rate and then multiply by the cost of the truck.

$$(1+0.0685) \cdot \$44,325$$
$$1.0685 \cdot \$44,325$$
$$\$47,361.26$$

This works because of something called the distributive property. When you're multiplying a number by the sum of two numbers, you can *distribute* the first number to both of those numbers and then add.

But hold on. It's easier to explain with variables.

$$a(b+c) = ab + ac$$

If we use the distributive property on the second method, we get the first method. Take a look:

$$(1+0.0685) \cdot \$44,325$$
$\$44,325(1+0.0685) \rightarrow$ switch the multiplication so that it looks like the distributive property
$(\$44,325 \cdot 1) + (\$44,325 \cdot 0.0685) \rightarrow$ distribute $\$44,325$
$\$44,325 + (\$44,325 \cdot 0.0685) \rightarrow$ and this is what the first method looks like

It's good to have choices.

Minty Fresh

Used cars are generally less expensive than new ones, unless you're deciding between a pre-owned Hummer and a brand new Hyundai, of course.

But how do dealer and automaker incentives stack up to buying used?

Check it out!

Roxanne is trying to decide between two cars. Her local dealership has a current model priced at $25,000, including tax. But online she saw the same car—pre-owned—for $15,000. The used car is in excellent condition and certified. Plus, the warranty transfers, so price is her only real consideration.

The dealership is offering free financing. And the automaker has a $2,000 cash-back program. That means she'll pay exactly $23,000 for the car and no interest at all.

But to finance the used car, she'll have to get a loan. To compare the prices, she'll need to find out how much she'll pay *in all* for the used car. That means she needs to know what interest on a loan will cost.

In order to calculate that, she'll need to know the principal (the amount she is borrowing and the basis of the interest calculation). That means the principal is $15,000. She'll also need to know the interest rate. Her bank is offering a 6% interest rate on car loans, for a period of 4 years. The interest is compounded annually, so once a year, the interest rate is calculated and added to the loan amount. So compounding interest means that in every year for the term of the loan, except the first year, Roxanne is paying interest on the interest she paid the year before (and the year before that . . . and you get the idea).

Roxanne can use an online calculator, or she can turn to a really simple formula:

$$A = P(1 + r)^n$$

Okay, breathe. It only *looks* hard. It's not difficult at all if you remember the order of operations—that is, what you do first, then second, and so on.

First, do anything inside the parentheses. Next, take care of exponents—those are the little numbers at the right top of another number. They tell how often to multiply the bigger number by itself. (So, 4^2 means $4 \cdot 4$, and 16^5 means $16 \cdot 16 \cdot 16 \cdot 16 \cdot 16$.) Then multiply or divide. And finally, add or subtract. In other words, Please Excuse My Dear Aunt Sally, or PEMDAS:

- **P**arentheses
- **E**xponents
- **M**ultiplication
- **D**ivision
- **A**ddition
- **S**ubtraction

Ready to apply this formula? With PEMDAS, you can do it!

A is the total amount she'll owe
P is the principal
r is the interest rate per compounding period
n is the number of compounding periods

Roxanne's principal (or the amount she's borrowing) is $15,000, so $P = \$15,000$. Her interest compounds yearly, so her rate is 6%. To make it easier to multiply, she can convert that percent to a decimal: $r = 6\% = 0.06$. And because the compounding period is annual, and the length of the loan is 4 years, $n = 4$.

$$A = \$15,000(1 + 0.06)^4$$
First add the numbers inside the parentheses.
$$A = \$15,000(1.06)^4$$
Now calculate the exponent. Remember, $1.06^4 = 1.06 \cdot 1.06 \cdot 1.06 \cdot 1.06$.
$$A = \$15,000(1.26)$$
Last step! Just multiply.
$$A = \$18,900$$

So, Roxanne would pay $18,900 total if she finances the purchase of the used car.

That's a heck of lot less than the $23,000 she'd pay for the new car. And she hasn't even figured in her down payment yet.

Why does that change anything? Because after making a down payment, she would be paying interest on less principal (remember, that's the amount she'll be borrowing). How would a $1,500 down payment affect her decision?

For the used car, she'd finance $13,500 instead of $15,000.

$A = \$13,500(1 + 0.06)^4$

$A = \$13,500 \cdot 1.26$

$A = \$17,010$

So the total she'll pay for the used car is $17,010.

And for the new car? She just needs to subtract her down payment from the adjusted price: $23,000 − $1,500, or $21,500.

Based on price alone, the new car doesn't seem so minty fresh.

Getting Down

If you're financing your car, you'll need to come up with a down payment, which is an upfront amount you pay before you can walk—or rather drive—off the lot with your new (or used) vehicle.

If you ask your grandfather how much to put down, he'll probably tell you at least 20% of the cost of the car. That was the typical down payment 40 years ago, and as it turns out, it's still good advice.

Melissa has her eye on a sweet little convertible with a price tag of $42,300. Her dad has offered to pay the 20% down payment. How large is the check he needs to write?

To find 20% of a number, you need to change the percent to a decimal and then multiply:

$$0.20 \cdot \$42,300 = \$8,460$$

Melissa can do this calculation easily by using a calculator. But could she also do it in her head? Yep, if she thinks of 20% as 10% times 2.

$$20\% = 10\% \cdot 2$$
$$10\% \text{ of } \$42,300 \text{ is } \$4,230$$
$$\$4,230 \cdot 2 = \$8,460$$

Either way, she needs a whopping $8,460 for her down payment.

But suppose Melissa has to cough up her own down payment, and she doesn't have as much cash stashed as her dad. How can she figure out how much car she can afford?

Let's say that Melissa has brown-bagged lunch and skipped dinners out for 2 years, just so that someday she could afford to buy a new car. At this point, she's put away $4,200. If she wants to use this for a 20% down payment on a new set of wheels, what's the most expensive car she can afford?

Here's another way of putting this question: 20% of what is $4,200?

If your brain is in math mode, you may automatically see an equation in which you need to find x. But if your brain is still focusing on whether that cute hatchback comes in robin's-egg blue, a little review is probably in order.

Luckily, there are some easy clues in the question itself:

- 20% is the same as 0.20
- when dealing with percents, *of* usually means multiplication
- *what* is the variable (the thing you need to find, or x)
- *is* means "equals"

When you recognize these clues, you can set up an algebraic equation (an equation to help you find x).

Wait! Don't close this book! It's not as hard as you think, so keep reading!

The 20% Rule

Why put down at least 20%? There's a one-word answer to that question: depreciation.

Depreciation is the value that the car loses over time. You can't buy a car for $40,000 and sell it for the same amount a year later. That's because as soon as a car is purchased, it depreciates in value. (Real estate is different. Buildings and land often appreciate—or gain value—over time.)

On average, a car's depreciation in the first year is 20%. If you've paid that much already with a down payment (and assuming you keep up-to-date on your payments), you will never be "upside-down" on your loan. In other words, you won't owe more on the car than it's worth.

That's a pretty big deal, if you suddenly hit hard times and need to sell your car. If you're upside-down, you will owe the bank the difference between the value of the car and the amount you've borrowed. That's the kind of math that no one wants to do.

20% of what is $4,200?

$$0.20 \cdot x = 4,200$$

$0.20x = 4,200$ (Remember, $0.20x$ is the same as 0.20 times x.)

Don't panic. Solving for x in this equation is really simple, if you remember three rules:

1. The object of the game is to get x all by itself on one side of the equals sign.

2. Whatever you do to one side of the equation, you must do to the other side to keep them even.

3. Division *undoes* multiplication.

With these rules in mind, can you guess what you need to do to find out what x is? How about if you divide each side of the equation by 0.20?

$$\frac{0.20x}{0.20} = \frac{4,200}{0.20}$$

When you divide $0.20x$ by 0.20, you get x—and remember that getting x by itself on one side of the equals sign is the key to solving the equation. Here's what you'll end up with:

$$x = 21,000$$

Whew! That's a lot of work to find out that with a $4,200 down payment, the most expensive car you can afford is one that costs $21,000. The good news is that there's an easier way: Just divide the down payment by the percent.

$$\$4,200 \div 20\% = \$4,200 \div 0.20 = \$21,000$$

So now you have two options for finding the down payment. You can remember to divide the down payment by the percent, or you can remember how to set up and solve a simple algebraic equation.

Month to Month

You might think you can afford a $21,000 vehicle, but if you're financing, it's smart to look at your monthly costs before you sign off on the deal.

On Balance

Whatever you do to one side of an equation, you have to do to the other side. But why? It's because of those two little horizontal, parallel lines: the equals sign.

Think of an equation as a teeter-totter. Let's say identical 8-year-old twins Truman and Nixon climb on—one on each side. Because they weigh the same, they can balance in mid-air. But if their older sister Reagan jumps on behind Nixon, the teeter-totter is no longer balanced.

Truman = Nixon

Truman ≠ Nixon + Reagan

The same thing happens with equations. Here's an easy one:

2 = 2

What happens when we add to one side of the equation only?

Does 2 = 2 + 1? Of course not.

2 ≠ 3

But if we do the same thing to both sides of the equation, we keep the balance.

2 = 2

Now, let's add the same thing to both sides of the equation.

Does 2 + 1 = 2 + 1?

Yes! 3 = 3

This works for any operation: addition, subtraction, multiplication, and division. Don't believe it? Try it out on your own.

If you can't afford the monthly payment, it doesn't matter how great a price you've negotiated.

Online calculators can help you find your monthly payment, but you can also figure it out on your own. Let's look at the formula. It's pretty ugly but not hard to use.

$$M = \frac{P\left(\dfrac{r}{12}\right)}{1 - \left(1 + \dfrac{r}{12}\right)^{-n}}$$

M is the monthly payment

P is the principal, or the total amount borrowed

r is the interest rate

n is the number of months in the loan

Dear Aunt Sally has her eye on a car that, with taxes, fees, and options, costs a nice, round $21,000. She can put down 20%, which is $4,200. That means she needs to finance $16,800. Before even setting foot on the lot, she contacted her bank and was approved for a 3-year loan with 4.5% interest.

Always organized, Aunt Sally first lists her variables—the letters that are in her formula and that change depending on how much she's borrowing, at what interest rate, and so on:

Principal	$16,800	$P = 16{,}800$
Rate	4.5%	$r = 0.045$
Number of months in the loan	36 months	$n = 36$

Now she can substitute.

$$M = \frac{16{,}800\left(\dfrac{0.045}{12}\right)}{1 - \left(1 + \dfrac{0.045}{12}\right)^{-36}}$$

"That's one doozy of an equation!" dear Aunt Sally exclaims. And then she gets to work, using PEMDAS. (Remember PEMDAS from earlier in the chapter?)

First she takes care of anything in parentheses:

$$M = \frac{16,800(0.00375)}{1-(1.00375)^{-36}}$$

Now she can take care of the exponent. She has a scientific calculator, so she just plugs in the numbers to find out that 1.000375^{-36} is 0.873. If she didn't have a scientific calculator, she could find one online (*www.calculator-tab.com* would be a good choice).

$$M = \frac{16,800(0.00375)}{1-0.873}$$

The rest of the calculations are pretty simple. She needs to multiply on the top and then subtract on the bottom.

$$M = \frac{63}{0.127}$$

Then she can divide, which will give her monthly payment.

$$M = 496.06$$

Dear Aunt Sally has discovered that her monthly car payment would be $496.06.

Phantom Parentheses

You may have wondered why Aunt Sally did all of the calculations in the numerator—the top part of the formula—and all of the calculations in the denominator—the bottom part of the formula—before she actually divided. That's because the parentheses in this situation were understood.

If she put all of the parentheses into the formula, it would look like this:

$$M = \frac{\left(P\left(\dfrac{r}{12}\right)\right)}{\left(1 - \left(1 + \dfrac{r}{12}\right)^{-n}\right)}$$

And that's an even uglier formula. It's much easier to consider the numerator of this formula as one part and the denominator as another part. The parentheses around each of those expressions are understood, so it is not necessary to write them.

That's a Negatory!

It may have been a long while since you last saw a negative exponent. Heck, it may have been so long ago that you don't remember ever seeing such a thing.

Negative exponents aren't so scary actually—if you know the rule that applies to them. A negative is just the inverse of a positive. Think of an inverse as turning something upside down. The inverse of addition is subtraction (the inverse of subtraction is addition). The inverse of multiplying is dividing.

$$x^{-y} = \frac{1}{x^y}$$

Don't hyperventilate. Compare the two sides of the equation to see what changed. First, the exponent (that little tiny y) is negative on the left-hand side of the equation and positive on the right-hand side. You didn't know how to deal with that negative exponent, so that's what you wanted, right? The other change explains how you got there. The entire thing is now the bottom number in a fraction with 1 on the top. Whew! Looks scary, but if you break it down, it's not so bad.

Let's just put some numbers in to illustrate:

$$8^{-2} = \frac{1}{8^2} = \frac{1}{64}$$

Or:

$$5^{-3} = \frac{1}{5^3} = \frac{1}{125}$$

Here's another way to think of it: Pretend that the exponent is positive and calculate it. Then divide your answer into 1.

Of course, with 0.00375^{-36} that rule doesn't much help—unless you want to multiply 0.00375 by itself 36 times and then divide it into 1. It's a much better plan to use a scientific or online calculator.

All in All

You may want to find the entire amount you'll pay for the car so that you'll know what you're getting into. In that case, you'll need to multiply the monthly payment by the number of months in the loan.

How much will dear Aunt Sally pay for her car over the life of the loan?

Her monthly payment is $496.06 on a 3-year loan. That means she'll make a monthly payment for 36 months.

$$\$496.06 \cdot 36 = \$17,858.16$$

Remember, she borrowed $16,800. That means she's paying an extra $1,058.16 ($17,858.16 – $16,800) for the privilege of financing her purchase.

Last But Not Lease

You've seen the commercials. To the tune of a well-worn 1970s rock song, a high-performance vehicle whips through hairpin turns with amazing dexterity. A deep-voiced announcer describes the car's precision handling, smooth ride, soft leather seats, and walnut interior.

"Starting at $55,699 dollars," the announcer croons. "Lease the new Agility for only $399 a month for 36 months."

Even if you're no geek, you may have wondered how the heck such an expensive car can have such a tiny monthly payment? The answer is easy: Leasing is way different from buying.

With a car lease, you'll have a lower monthly payment and a shorter term. At the end of that period, you can either give the car back or buy it outright. That's because you're merely *leasing* (renting) the vehicle; it doesn't belong to you.

When you lease a vehicle, you agree to pay a fee if you drive it over a prescribed number of miles. You also have to be careful not to damage the car or cause unnecessary wear and tear.

This is why leases aren't great options for moms with 30-mile one-way commutes and sticky-fingered kids who drink from sippy-cups full of milk that invariably roll under the seat undetected.

The other thing to consider is how well the car retains its value. Leases work best with vehicles that keep their value—which is why they're used most commonly by Mercedes and Jaguar drivers.

Still, leasing is a great option for many drivers. And if you fit in that category, it's a smart idea to do some figuring before you stroll into the showroom.

The lease itself has a bunch of parts:

1. The *cap cost* or *lease price* is the price you've negotiated, so it should be less than the sticker price. Otherwise, you should just buy the car.
2. The *lease term* is the length of time that you'll have the lease. It should be no longer than the warranty that comes with the vehicle. That's because you don't want your warranty to run out before your lease is up. Who wants to be responsible for repairs on a car she or he doesn't own?
3. The *residual value* is what the vehicle is worth at the end of the lease period. This is usually expressed as a percent. Thus a car may have a 60% residual value at the end of 36 months. That means the car has an estimated depreciation of 40% (100% − 60%) over 3 years.
4. The *money factor* is basically the interest you'll pay. Leasing a car is not like leasing a house, because, unlike real estate, cars lose value over time. (If it's any consolation, equipment leases, such as leases on a backhoe or a copier, involve interest too.) But the money factor is not exactly interest, because with a car lease, you're paying for the depreciation of the value of the car.

There will probably be other things to consider—such as dealer fees. Because those vary so much, we'll leave them out of our calculations here. But you should research car leases in your area, and with each particular dealer and lender, before parking yourself on the other side of a car salesperson's desk.

Once you've agreed on a lease price for the car, the dealer will present you with a calculation of your monthly lease payment. But it's important to know how to make this calculation yourself, so you can catch any errors the dealer might make (and to ask about any added extras you don't understand and didn't anticipate). Knowing exactly what is going on may also give you an edge in negotiations.

$$\text{Monthly lease payment} =$$
$$\text{depreciation fee} + \text{finance fee} + \text{sales tax}$$

Instead of creating a really huge formula, it makes more sense to break this problem down into its three parts. You'll just need to remember to add the three together at the end.

$$\text{Depreciation fee} = (\text{cap cost} - \text{residual value}) \div \text{lease term}$$
$$\text{Finance fee} = (\text{cap cost} - \text{residual value}) \bullet \text{money factor}$$
$$\text{Sales tax} = \text{monthly payment} \bullet \text{sale tax rate}$$

Crystal is in the market for a new car. Multistep problems like these can blow her mind. But as a professional organizer, she lives by the adage "A place for everything and everything in its place."

Therefore, when she decided to lease her next vehicle—and to do some of the math before she waltzed into the showroom—she sat at her immaculate desk with a calculator, a printed description of the financing she thought she could get, and a stack of clean, crisp paper.

At the top of one paper she wrote "Depreciation Fee" and then its formula. On the second she wrote "Finance Fee" and its formula. And on the third she wrote "Sales Tax" and its formula. Then she turned to the "Depreciation Fee" paper and ignored the others.

To find the depreciation fee, she needs to know the cap cost, residual value, and lease term. In the language of math,

$$D = (c - r) \div t$$

The last two values come from the research Crystal has done on financing. The car she wants has a 70% residual value over 3 years.

Although she knows the sticker price and the residual value percent, Crystal doesn't know the residual value yet. Because the residual value is a percent of the sticker price, she just needs to multiply.

$$\text{Residual value} = \text{sticker price} \cdot \text{residual value percent}$$
$$\text{Residual value} = \$36{,}890 \cdot 0.70$$
$$\text{Residual value} = \$25{,}823$$

Now she has the residual value and the term. She needs to know the cap cost (lease price) of the vehicle.

Crystal, who is a great negotiator, thinks she could get the dealership down from a sticker price of $36,890 to $35,350. So, she writes two more figures on her paper:

$$\text{Sticker price} = \$36{,}890$$
$$\text{Cap cost (or lease price)} = \$35{,}350$$

She circles three numbers on her page: The lease term (36 months), the cap cost ($35,350), and the residual value ($25,823). These are the numbers that she'll use in her formula.

$$\text{Depreciation fee} = (\text{cap cost} - \text{residual value}) \div \text{lease term, or}$$
$$D = (c - r) \div t$$

She plugs her numbers in to get

$$D = (\$35{,}350 - \$25{,}823) \div 36$$

She remembers that she needs to calculate what's in the parentheses first:

$$D = \$9{,}527 \div 36$$

Then she arrives at

$$D = \$264.64$$

She highlights the depreciation fee and sets this paper aside.

Now Crystal can find the finance fee—or the amount she'll pay the leasing company for financing the lease. She turns her attention to that paper, looking at the formula

$$\text{Finance fee} = (\text{cap cost} - \text{residual value}) \bullet \text{money factor, or}$$
$$F = (c - r) \bullet f$$

She knows the cap cost is $35,350 and the residual value is $25,823. She looks over the research she's done on her financing and reads that she can get a financing package with a 0.00295 money factor. (Remember, *money factor* is like interest. It works a little differently, but if Crystal thinks of it as interest, she can get a good idea of how much she'll pay for a car lease.)

$$\text{Finance fee} = (\$35,350 - \$25,823) \bullet 0.00295$$
$$\text{Finance fee} = \$9,527 \bullet 0.00295$$
$$\text{Finance fee} = \$28.10$$

She highlights this figure and moves on to her last piece of paper:

$$\text{Sales tax} = \text{monthly payment} \bullet \text{sale tax rate, or } S = p \bullet t$$

But Crystal doesn't know her monthly payment yet, does she? Because she's über-organized, it's easy enough to find. All she needs to do is add the two numbers that are highlighted on the other pieces of paper: the depreciation fee and the finance fee.

$$\text{Monthly payment} = \text{depreciation fee} + \text{finance fee}$$
$$\text{Monthly payment} = \$264.64 + \$28.10$$
$$\text{Monthly payment} = \$292.74$$

Crystal lives in Illinois, so her sales tax rate is 6.25%. Now she can finally use the formula

$$\text{Sales tax} = \text{monthly payment} \cdot \text{sale tax rate, or } S = p \cdot t$$
$$S = \$292.74 \cdot 0.0625$$
$$\text{Sales tax} = \$18.30$$

She highlights the sales tax and then reaches for a clean sheet of paper. At the top, she writes the formula for finding the monthly lease payment:

$$\text{Monthly lease payment} =$$
$$\text{depreciation fee} + \text{finance fee} + \text{sales tax, or } P = D + F + S$$

She reviews the other three pieces of paper, in order to be sure that she's found all of the components. Then she begins plugging in the values:

$$P = \$264.64 + \$28.10 + \$18.30$$
$$\text{Monthly lease payment} = \$311.04$$

Crystal circles this figure three times, gathers all of her papers and staples them. She tucks these into a crisp, new folder, types "Monthly Lease Payment Calculations" into her handy-dandy label maker, prints the label, and sticks it on the folder tab. Her purse and keys are helpfully hanging by the back door, so she grabs them and heads out to the car dealership—confident that she'll be able to make a good deal.

After all, information—and organization—is power.

Lease or Buy?

Because Crystal's life is so organized and her clients are local, leasing is probably a good option for her. How much is she saving each month over the monthly cost of buying the car outright?

Let's say Crystal is able to finance the car over 5 years at 4% interest. Using the monthly payment formula reveals that her monthly payment would be $651.02.

That's more than twice her monthly payment on the lease!

$$\$651.02 - \$311.04 = \$339.98$$

But remember that by leasing, Crystal will never own the car outright, and she'll always have a car payment.

Then there's the mileage restriction. If, in any year, Crystal goes over her allotted miles—which may be as few as 12,000 miles—she will have to pay up to 25¢ per mile. Thus if she drives the car 16,000 miles, she'll owe as much as $1,000—or more than 2 months' worth of lease payments.

The bottom line? Crystal will be responsible for the car during its most expensive years.

Problems with Problem Solving

Deciding whether to buy or lease a car can seem overwhelming. And one of the reasons for this is that the math is complex. Finding the monthly payment on a loan or a lease requires the organizational skills of Martha Stewart! So if you're more like Jack Black, here's some help. Remember, multistep problems can be easier to solve if you ask a few simple questions.

1. What do you have?
   List the information that you know. That includes any formulas you may need to use and the numbers that may be plugged into those formulas.
2. What do you want?
   Write down the goal of the problem—finding the monthly payment or finding how much you can afford.

3. What can you do to make things easier?

   No, the answer isn't "get someone else to do it"! Here are some simple ideas: Draw a picture, make a chart, act out the problem, look for a pattern, list rules (like PEMDAS). And don't forget to toss out any information that you don't need. You won't necessarily use every single number that you have.

4. Does the solution make sense?

When you find the solution, be sure to check it out. In other words, know what makes a reasonable answer.

Let's say you're trying to find the monthly payment on a $12,900 car loan. If you come up with $14,358.98, you've probably made a mistake somewhere along the line. Unless you've got the worst car loan in history, you're not going to pay more than the car is worth each month. Likewise, if you find that your monthly payment is only $76.34, you may want to take another look at your calculations. It would be nice to have such a low monthly payment, but that's not likely, given the price you are paying for the car.

On the Market: Buying a House by the Numbers

It's the American dream. Perhaps you're in the market for a house in the 'burbs with a picket fence and a big front porch. Or maybe you're a city mouse, looking for shelter among row houses or modern condos. Heck, you could even be considering roughing it off the grid in a modest cabin in the woods.

Unless you're renting a studio apartment in the Big Apple or are content living in your parents' basement, buying a home is probably on your list of things to do as a grownup. But stepping into the real estate market can feel like jumping out of a perfectly good airplane. It's downright scary.

That's because most folks don't have hundreds of thousands of dollars lying around. And that means one simple thing: When you buy a house, you agree to make a monthly mortgage payment.

Houses have big price tags. And mortgages are long-term commitments. But a few figures can give you the confidence to pull that parachute cord at just the right moment—and land safely on your feet.

Throwing Down

You can't get something for nothing, right? At least that's what your mama always told you. And that's why she wouldn't approve of a zero-down mortgage.

Unless you're a veteran with a Veterans Administration loan, you should expect to make a down payment on your house. And not just to please good old mom. The fact is, she has good reason to be suspicious of zero-down mortgages. When you skip the down payment, you're borrowing a larger chunk of cash, which means a bigger monthly bill from your lender. But even worse is not having any equity in your home when you move in. If the real estate market goes south, you could find yourself "upside-down" on your mortgage—that is, owing more than the property is worth. In other words, if you had to sell your house, you wouldn't get enough to pay back your lender. And that's a scary situation.

Lenders really like down payments, too. Down payments say, "These buyers are trustworthy. They know how to save money. They're serious about buying a house."

But down payments are not just great for wooing the perfect lender. They also lower your monthly payment—which in turn lowers the amount of money that you'll pay in interest on the loan *and* the total amount you'll be shelling out over the life of the loan.

In short, making a $40,000 down payment up front can save you big bucks over 30 years.

Are you convinced yet?

There's another reason to make a large down payment: private mortgage insurance, or PMI. Remember, your down payment says, "You can trust me." A big down payment means the lender can *really* trust you. If you don't have at least 20% to put down, your lender will require that you pay a little extra each month for insurance on your loan. This protects the lender in case you don't make your house payments.

Just like a down payment on a car, the down payment on a house is a percent of the total price of the house. And just as in the purchase of a car, the amount you have for your down payment is one of the things that will affect how much house you can afford.

An example will probably help.

It's been 10 years since you graduated. You have a great job and your college loans are all paid off. It's time to take the next step: buying a house. You've been saving your bonuses for 7 years, and your latest bank statement shows a balance of $16,790. But by a stroke of good luck, that's not all you have.

Nobody thought that ugly painting from your Aunt Martha was worth a thing, but you had a hunch. So when the popular television program, *Your Trash, My Treasure* came to town, you and a fraternity brother hauled it down to be appraised. Turns out you've got a good eye, because the darned thing is valued at about $40,000. Within a week, you sold it to a collector for $35,770.

With your savings, you have $52,560—that's $16,790 plus $35,770. Looks like a great down payment on a house.

But how much house can you afford? Clearly, you're no dummy, so you're shooting for a 20% down payment.

20% of what is $52,560?

In Chapter 2, we talked about how to answer this question. If you've already read that chapter, you may remember that there are two ways to approach this problem: You can create and solve an algebraic equation, or you can remember a simple division problem.

If you don't remember the shortcut, never fear. The algebra in this problem is very simple. All you need to do is remember some key terms. *Of* means multiplication; *what* is the variable (the answer you're looking for); and *is* means "equals." Translating and putting it all together, you get this equation:

$$0.20x = \$52,560$$

To find x, you need to isolate it. That means you need to undo the multiplication. And to undo the multiplication, you need to do the inverse operation. Remember what *inverse* means? It means the opposite of something. Because the opposite of multiplication is division, that's what you need to do. Simply divide each side of the equation by 0.20.

$$\frac{0.20x}{0.20} = \frac{52,560}{0.20}$$
$$x = \$262,800$$

With a $52,560 down payment, then, you can afford to purchase a $262,800 house.

Now do you remember the shortcut? Just divide the down payment by the percent. (Hey! That's what you did to solve the equation!)

You can use also the shortcut to figure out what you could afford if you only paid 10% down.

$$\$52,560 \div 0.10 = \$525,600$$

So, if you put 10% down, you can afford almost twice as much house, or a home worth $525,600. But be careful! There's a heck of a lot more that goes into the mortgage. If you borrow more money, your monthly payment will be much higher.

Being Equitable

In real estate, *equity* isn't the union for professional stage actors. Nope, finding the equity you have in your home boils down to solving a simple subtraction problem:

Equity = the market value of the property – the outstanding mortgage balance

Unlike a car or a couch or anything else you might buy, real estate often appreciates in value. That's why real estate is considered an investment—you may well earn money when you buy and later sell a house.

Down payments affect your equity. When you can make a large down payment, you reduce the amount of money you owe on the property. That means you have more equity from the very beginning.

Quite literally, make a $20,000 down payment on a house, you will have $20,000 in equity before you even move in!

That is a huge deal, especially if the real estate market goes south. If you need to sell your house quickly, but values have gone down, it helps to have some equity. At the very least, you may be able to break even—a much better deal than taking a loss. Having equity also enables you to take out a second mortgage, if you need to remodel or update your house. And if you wish to refinance your mortgage at a lower rate a few years down the road, having extra equity will help make that possible.

The Bottom Line

Before you even start shopping for a house, you'd better have a budget in mind; otherwise, you might find yourself looking around in a neighborhood that's too rich for your bank account. Luckily, one little multiplication rule will help you estimate how much house you can afford.

It turns out that you should shoot for no more than five times your annual gross salary. If you gross $65,700 a year, for instance, your top limit should be 5 • $65,700, or $328,500. (And if your spouse or partner is also contributing to the family budget, you can add his or her salary, as well.)

Another important thing to consider is the current economy. In a poor economy, you should probably budget a smaller amount, just in case you get caught with a lower-paying job or, worse, with no job at all. And regardless of the economy, you should always consider how much debt you have. Not much? You may be able to handle a larger mortgage. A lot of debt? Do yourself a big favor and aim lower.

Month to Month

Gleaming hardwood floors, an attached garage, and a spectacular master suite may be the main attractions, but if you want to live in it, you have to be able to afford it. Forget the bells and whistles; you need a house with a monthly payment you can live with.

Naima has had enough of her neighbors' loud music, loud parties, and loud arguments. It's time for her to move out of the apartment complex she's lived in since she left home after high school. She is more than ready for the peace and quiet of a single-family home and a little distance from her neighbors.

But can she afford to buy? Her monthly rent is $950, and with her recent promotion at work, she can add an additional $300 to that payment each month. Naima needs a monthly mortgage payment of no more than $1,250.

She has $17,450 in the bank for a down payment, and she's prequalified for a loan: a 30-year mortgage with 4.25% fixed-rate interest. It was important for her to get prequalified for her mortgage, because the interest rate and the term (time period) of the loan play a part in how much she can afford. With a higher interest rate or a shorter time period, she could afford less. That's because these factors increase the monthly mortgage payments.

Knowing that she can afford a monthly mortgage payment of $1,250, how much house can she buy without exceeding her monthly budget?

Naima can use one of hundreds of online mortgage calculators to figure this out. But she's old school, and so she turns to the loan formula:

$$P = M\left(\frac{(1+r)^n - 1}{r(1+r)^n}\right)$$

P=principal (the amount of the loan)
M=monthly payment
r=monthly interest rate
n=number of months in the loan

Even though you're only working with a couple of variables here, you may get tripped up in a couple of places if you're not paying attention. First, r is the *monthly* interest rate, and Naima was quoted a *yearly* rate. Therefore, she needs to divide 4.25% by 12 to get r.

r=yearly mortgage rate÷12
r=4.25%÷12
r=0.0425÷12 (Convert the percent to a decimal.)
r=0.0035

The number of months in the loan, or n, is another potential pitfall. Naima has a 30-year mortgage, but she needs to come up with the number of months:

n=number of years•12
n=30•12
n=360

Here's what Naima knows:

M=\$1,250
r=0.0035
n=360

It's an ugly formula, for sure, but Naima buckles down and gives it a shot. She plugs in her variables first:

$$P = 1{,}250\left(\frac{(1+0.0035)^{360} - 1}{0.0035(1+0.0035)^{360}} \right)$$

Remembering the order of operations (PEMDAS, or Please Excuse My Dear Aunt Sally), Naima knows that she must deal with what's in parentheses first. So, she gives her full attention to the fraction part of the formula. Looking closer, she adds within the smaller parentheses.

$$P = 1,250 \left(\frac{(1+0.0035)^{360} - 1}{0.0035(1.0035)^{360}} \right)$$

Now she looks for exponents. Only a math prodigy can find the 360th power of a number without a calculator, but last year Naima gave her scientific calculator to her younger brother, who is now taking Algebra II. She grabs her laptop and finds a free online calculator by searching for "free scientific calculator." A couple of clicks later, she has more information for her formula:

$$P = 1,250 \left(\frac{3.5177 - 1}{0.0035(3.5177)} \right)$$

Now the calculations are pretty simple. She subtracts in the numerator (that's the top number) and then multiplies in the denominator (that's the bottom number).

$$P = 1,250 \left(\frac{2.5177}{0.0123} \right)$$

Naima can finish the last two operations quickly. She divides the numbers in the parentheses and then multiplies.

$$P = 1,250 \cdot 204.6911$$
$$P = \$255,863.87$$

The loan formula shows that Naima can afford the monthly payments on a house priced at $255,863.87. This is based on what she can spend each month on a mortgage payment, as well as the interest rate her lender can offer. But is her answer right? Well, not quite.

Remember that Naima has a down payment of $17,450. Using the loan formula, she found out that she can afford a house priced at $255,863.87, but that doesn't take her down payment into consideration. Actually, she can afford to buy a house priced at $255,863.87 + $17,450, or $273,313.87.

Quiet living, here she comes.

PITI the Fool

You may be looking for the simple life, but you're not going to find it in your monthly mortgage payment. That's because the monthly check that you write to your mortgage company includes more than just a payment toward principal and interest.

A monthly mortgage payment usually has four parts. These parts are called PITI, for Principal, Interest, Taxes, Insurance.

- The *principal* is the amount that you borrowed. In the early years of the mortgage, you'll pay only a little bit of the principal each month, and most of your payment will go toward interest. That's because the bank wants its cut as soon as possible. As the mortgage ages, the principal portion of your monthly payment grows. (But don't worry; if you have a fixed-rate mortgage, your monthly payment will stay the same.)

- And then there's a little something called *interest*. In return for the loan, you agree to pay the lender (probably a bank or mortgage company) a percent of the price of the house each month. This interest is compounded—which means the interest earns interest.

Dying for a Loan

The word *mortgage* was probably coined in the fourteenth century. It's an Old French word that literally means "death pledge."

But that doesn't mean that a mortgage will kill you. *Au contraire.* With a mortgage, the debt dies when it's paid. In other words, you can get out of a mortgage in one of two ways—by paying it off or by refinancing with another loan.

Extra! Extra!

The beauty of renting is that someone else takes care of maintenance and repairs. So who's responsible for those costs when you buy a house? That would be you.

The water heater breaks? Either you replace it or you take cold showers. A giant icicle brings down the gutters along the entire east side of your roof? You'll be paying the gutter guys. A family of birds takes up residence in your bathroom fan? You guessed it. You're in charge of evicting your feathered friends and installing a new fan.

Real estate experts estimate that these costs will average 1% to 2% of the value of the home each year. So if the home you're planning to buy costs $189,000, you can expect to pay between $1,890 and $3,780 for maintenance and repairs each year.

Unless, of course, you bought that fixer-upper. In that case, you're probably on the hook for a whole lot more.

(Note that the formula Naima used includes only principal and interest. The taxes and insurance have to be figured in later, because they vary so widely from place to place.)

- Property or real estate *taxes* also make your monthly payment add up. State and local governments charge these taxes to pay for everything from new roads to schools. The tax bill is due on an annual or semiannual basis, but your lender may offer to pay these for you each year, which enables you to spread this cost month to month—and adds the cost to your monthly mortgage payment.
- Finally, there's *insurance*. Your homeowner's insurance can be rolled into the monthly mortgage payment. Your lender will almost certainly require you to carry homeowner's insurance in order to qualify for the loan. And if you didn't put down at least 20%, you'll also pay private mortgage insurance (PMI).

Interesting, *Very* Interesting

Okay, houses are expensive. That's not difficult to understand. But you might be shocked by how much you pay for a home over the life of the mortgage.

That's because the interest on a mortgage is *compounded*. In other words, you pay interest on the interest.

Here's how it works, using some very simple numbers. Let's say you've borrowed $1,000 at 10% interest that is compounded monthly. And let's also say that your lender has agreed that you can pay $150 each month to pay off that loan. In the first month of the loan, you will owe $1,000 plus 10% interest, or $100. So, the total you will owe in that month is $1,100.

But that's not what your lender expects you to pay that month. Remember, your monthly payment is $150. You make that payment, which means you still owe $950 (because $1,100−$150=$950).

The next month rolls around, and you need to make a payment. But do you owe $950? Nope. That's because interest has been calculated again. Ten percent of $950 is $95, so your total debt has risen again: $950+$95=$1,045. After making your $150 payment, you owe $895 (because $1,045−$150=$895).

And so it goes every single month. The lender adds interest, and you make a payment. But you are always paying interest on the interest.

Drew bought a house almost 30 years ago. In fact, he's about to make the very last payment of $608—the same check he's been writing for the last 359 months. His original mortgage was $120,358. Just for kicks, he'd like to know how much he paid in interest over the life of the loan.

Each month, $20 of the payment goes to cover taxes, so Drew's mortgage lender has received $588 per month for 30 years. (Drew decided not to include his home insurance in his monthly mortgage payment, so the insurance part of PITI is not a factor.) What was the total that Drew paid to his lender? He can use the total mortgage formula to find out:

$$T = Mn$$

T is the total of the loan payments
M is the monthly payments
n is the total number of payments over the life of the mortgage

Remember, there are 12 months in a year, and Drew made a mortgage payment each and every month for 30 years. So, he made a total of 360 payments.

$$T = \$588 \cdot 360$$
$$T = \$211,680$$

Because Drew originally borrowed $120,358, how much interest has he paid over the life of the mortgage?

$$\$211,680 - \$120,358 = \$91,322$$

Would someone please get Drew a chair? He looks a little woozy.

If Drew had taken out a 15-year loan, he'd have paid it off long, long ago. And he wouldn't have paid as much interest. The shorter the term of the loan, the less interest is paid on interest.

You know that the longer the mortgage, the smaller the monthly payment. But the length of the mortgage also affects the total amount that you'll pay.

Here's how it works mathematically.

Let's say that Drew bought his house using a 15-year mortgage with a 4.5% fixed-rate. And remember, he bought the house for $120,358.

Using a trustworthy online calculator, Drew finds that his monthly payment on a 15-year mortgage would have been $920.73. This payment is higher than the payment he owed with his 30-year mortgage, but that's because he wouldn't be taking so long to pay it off.

With a 15-year mortgage, he would have made 180 monthly payments ($15 \cdot 12$), so the total payment would have been

$$\$920.73 \cdot 180$$
$$\$165,731.40$$

How much would Drew have saved if he'd gone with a 15-year mortgage? All he needs to do to find out is subtract the total paid for the 15-year mortgage from the total paid for the 30-year mortgage.

$$\$211,680 - \$165,731.40$$
$$\$45,948.60$$

By spreading out his mortgage payments over 30 years, instead of 15 years, Drew ended up paying almost $50,000 more. That's more than most people earn in a year!

(How about if we don't tell Drew. In this case, ignorance is bliss.)

What's Your Rate?

When you shop for a mortgage—or any kind of loan, for that matter—you should listen for three little magic letters: APR, which stands for annual percentage rate. That's the number most often associated with mortgages and other loans.

When a newspaper article touts mortgage rates at 4.5%, that's the APR. And when you see a commercial that advertises a car dealer's 6% financing, that's the APR.

The A for "annual" is the star here. Any third grader can tell you that *annual* means something that happens once a year. But mortgages and other loans are usually compounded monthly. That means the interest is calculated each month and added to the balance of the loan. (You're paying interest on the interest.)

And this means you need to be careful with your formulas. The r in a formula may stand for the APR, or it may represent the interest rate per month.

This all comes down to *reasonable answers*. Everybody makes mistakes. Everybody misunderstands things from time to time. When you put everything into a formula and come up with an answer that doesn't make sense, go back.

Unless you've got the world's worst mortgage, you shouldn't be paying $123,450 a month on a $100,000 house.

When Rates Go Up and Down

It's terrific if you can get a fixed interest rate. That means your interest rate won't go up—or down—for the life of the loan. But with some mortgages, the interest rate won't stay put. These are called adjustable-rate mortgages, or ARMs.

With an ARM, the initial interest rate stays the same for a specified period of time. Then it will periodically go up or down.

- 1-1 ARM: fixed rate for 1 year, adjusts every year after that
- 3-1 ARM: fixed rate for 3 years, adjusts every year after that
- 5-1 ARM: fixed rate for 5 years, adjusts every year after that

But where do these adjustments come from? Can the mortgage lender simply jack up the rate from 6% to 20%? No way.

Changes in interest rates are dictated by something called an economic index. There are dozens of economic indices (the plural of *index*) so it's a good idea to consider which one the lender is using when you're shopping for an ARM. Fluctuations in rates are affected by a variety of forces, including the health of the economy, as well as supply and demand. For example, when the number of houses on the market is up and the economy is down, rates are typically lower.

Every ARM will have an interest cap, or a limit on how high the interest can get. This may be a periodic cap (a limit on the amount the interest rate can increase from period to period) or an overall cap (a limit on the amount the rate can increase over the life of the mortgage). If you had an ARM with a periodic interest rate cap of 2%, your interest could not go up more than 2% each adjustment period. So, if your interest rate were 8%, the highest it could get in the next adjustment period would be 10%. And in this example, if you had an ARM with an overall cap of 5%, your interest rate would *never* go over 13% (or 8% + 5%).

The interest rate of an ARM also includes something called the *margin*. This is an extra charge that the lender adds on to the rate to cover its costs and profits. Good news! Unlike interest rates, on an adjustable-rate mortgage, margins usually stay the same over the life of the loan.

Here's the bottom line: When you have an ARM, your monthly payments can change. This should make perfect sense. If interest is part of your monthly payment, changes in the interest rate will make the payment go up or down.

Why would anyone want a mortgage with monthly payments that might fluctuate from year to year?

A lot of times, the initial rate for an ARM is less than what you can get for a fixed-rate mortgage. If you don't expect to own the house for very long, you can save big bucks with an ARM. And lower interest rates mean lower monthly payments. So you could afford pricier digs with an ARM.

Finally, any increases in your income can cover higher monthly payments. So if you're expecting a big pay raise or a higher-paying job, an ARM might be a good option.

The Incredibly Shrinking Total

You don't have to spring for a short-term mortgage to reduce the total you pay for your house. And guess what? The total-payment formula shows you how.

$$T = Mn$$

Remember that equations are like teeter-totters—the equals sign means the sides must be balanced. So if you want T to be smaller, Mn must be smaller too, right?

In any loan, there are three variables that affect how much your monthly payments are (and also how much your total payment is). We talked about this in Chapter 2, but to review, here they are:

P is the principal, or the amount borrowed
r is the monthly interest rate
n is the number of months in the loan

If you can reduce any of these, you will reduce the total loan payment.

To reduce the principal, you can buy a different house, negotiate a lower price, or increase the size of your down payment. We'll leave that up to you (and your real estate agent). But you can also reduce the monthly interest rate and the number of months in the loan in other ways.

First, let's look at the interest rate. Just like looking for the best deal on a car or a flat-screen TV, you want to shop around. The lower the interest rate, the less you'll pay on the loan altogether.

Prove it, you say? Here's an example. Let's say you're borrowing $325,000 to buy a house. You have the choice of two 30-year mortgages—one has a 6.25% interest rate and one that has a 6.75% rate. To find out how much you would pay for either loan, you can use a formula, or you can turn to an online mortgage calculator. Let's make things easy this time with an online mortgage calculator.

You'll pay $2,001.08 each month for the first mortgage (the one with a 6.25% interest rate). That's a total of $720,388.80 over the life of the mortgage. And you'll pay $2,107.94 each month for the second mortgage (the one with a 6.75% interest rate)—a whopping $758,858.40 over the life of the mortgage.

That tiny difference in the interest rate adds up to a huge difference in the end.

But there's another way to limit the amount you'll pay in interest. When you buy a home, you'll probably have the option of buying points (sometimes called discount points), which is essentially a way to prepay the interest rate. You pay for points when you sign the final mortgage contracts. Why would you do that, you ask?

When you buy discount points, you lower the interest rate on your mortgage. How nifty is that?

Each discount point costs 1% of the mortgage amount and lowers the interest rate on a 30-year fixed rate mortgage by about 0.125% (or $\frac{1}{8}$ of 1%), although this can vary.

Buying a point (or two points or ten points) is even more valuable than it sounds.

Let's look at an example with nice, round numbers.

To buy the house you've got your eye on, you'll have to take out a mortgage loan for $100,000. Because a discount point equals 1% of the loan amount, each point costs $1,000. If you have a 30-year fixed-rate mortgage with 7.5% interest, purchasing one point will lower your rate to 7.375%. (That's because $7.5\% - 0.125\% = 7.375\%$.)

Using a mortgage calculator, you can find that buying a point reduces your monthly mortgage payment from $699.21 to $690.68, leaving you with an extra $8.53 in your pocket every month.

That doesn't seem like a lot of money, but over the life of the mortgage, it can add up! Even in the first year, you would save $8.53 • 12, or $102.36.

And over the life of the mortgage, you would save $8.53 • 360, or $3,070.80. (Remember, there are 360 months in 30 years.)

In short, when you reduce r, you can lower your total payment.

What else can you change? That's right—n.

You can do this a couple different ways, but they all boil down to one thing—paying off your mortgage early. It turns out that there's a really crafty way to do this. See if you can figure this out by answering some very simple questions.

1. How many months are there in a year?
2. How many weeks are there in a year?

Most mortgages are paid monthly. Because there are 12 months in the year, you make 12 payments a year. However, if you made your mortgage payment every 4 weeks instead of every month, you'd make 13 payments a year (52 weeks ÷ 4 = 13). What many people do is split their monthly payment in half and pay that half-payment every 2 weeks. (This works especially well for people who get paid every 2 weeks instead of on fixed days of the month). Thus, if your mortgage payment were $1,000 per month, and you paid $500 every 2 weeks, you'd make 26 half-payments in the year, or 13 full payments.

That's an extra mortgage payment each and every year.

Here's the math:

Hannah has a monthly mortgage payment of $1,300. That means she pays $15,600 each year for her mortgage.

If she decides to make biweekly payments instead, she'll send in $650 every other week. That translates to 26 payments of $650 each year, for a total of $16,900.

That's $1,300 more a year than Hannah is paying with monthly payments, which means she'll pay off her mortgage faster.

It's not like you're tricking the bank with these payments. You're actually tricking yourself, by spreading out an extra monthly payment over the entire year. For most folks, that's a heck of a lot easier than writing an extra check at the end of the year. *Note:* Some loans don't allow prepayment (which is what this essentially is) or impose penalties for prepayment, so make sure your mortgage terms allow you to do this.

A Pointed Question

Just because you can buy points, should you? Well, of course not.

First, you need to know whether the savings will be more than the cost. If you buy a point for $1,000 and save $2,948.40, you'll end up pocketing $1,948.40. (Which could very well be worth it.)

Another thing to consider is the break-even place. That's the number of months you must keep the loan to break even on paying points. This calculation is pretty simple: Just divide the amount charged for discount points by the monthly savings.

For example, if you paid $1,000 for a point to save $8.19 per month, your break-even place would be

$$\$1,000 \div 8.19$$
$$122.1$$

This means that your points purchase will "pay off" if you keep the loan for *more than* 122 months (or 10 years 2 months).

And if the time to your break-even place is longer than the life of the loan? That's a pretty obvious indication that spending so much on points is just not worth it.

Points or Down Payment?

When you buy discount points, you pay for them in one lump sum, at the closing. So why not put that money toward the down payment instead?

You may want to think about that—and here are some questions that can help:

1. *How long will you be in the house?* If you're planning to sell your house before you break even, adding to your down payment makes more sense. However, if you're planning to keep the mortgage for a long time, buying points may be the better option.
2. *Do you need a tax deduction?* Uncle Sam offers an incentive for buying points: As of this writing, you can deduct the entire cost of discount points from your taxes in the year that you buy your house. Otherwise, that deduction is spread out over the time that you have the mortgage. So, if you need a tax deduction right away, buy the points.
3. *Do you have enough money for the down payment?* Some lenders require a 20% down payment, so you may not have a choice at all.
4. *Will a larger down payment affect the type of loan you can get?* If you want a 30-year fixed-rate loan, you'll probably need to make a large down payment.
5. *Which will lower your monthly payments more: increasing your down payment or buying points?* A little bit of math can help you keep some cash in the bank (or under your mattress).

At the Closing

When you close on the purchase of a house, bring your checkbook. Unless you've negotiated something different with the seller, you'll have to lay down some cash before the deal is done.

Here are some of the costs you might be expected to cover at closing:

- *Processing fees* cover the administrative costs of processing your loan. These include expenses incurred in checking your credit report, the lender's attorney's fees, document preparation costs, and so on.
- You already know what *points* are: a one-time charge that you may pay in order to lower your interest rate over the life of the mortgage.
- An *appraisal fee* is charged when your lender needs to establish the actual value of the home.
- The *title fee* covers the cost of ensuring that the home belongs to the seller, a process called a title search. This fee may also include title insurance, which protects the lender against an error in the title search.

How can you figure out what all of these costs will add up to? Fortunately, the Real Estate Settlement Procedures Act (RESPA) requires that all lenders give the borrower a Good Faith Estimate (GFE) of all the fees associated with the loan. This way, you will have a general idea of how much you'll need to pay in closing costs.

But as the name suggests, a Good Faith Estimate is just that—an estimate. The actual fee may be slightly lower or higher.

At Home: Will Your New Fridge Fit?

Ah! Home sweet home! Even if you're not inclined to watch marathons of *This Old House* on PBS, sprucing up your digs can be a rewarding experience.

Except when it isn't.

Simple projects like painting a room or hanging curtains can become complicated—and expensive—math problems. How much paint do you need? Where should you hang the curtain rods so that the drapes "puddle" just as they do on the cover of *Home Interiors* magazine?

Math probably can't help you pick out the perfect shade of green for a south-facing room, but it does factor in the economics and geometry of home improvement.

So grab your confidence and a tape measure and get started!

Color Your World

Narcissa is so ready to redecorate her bedroom. Against their better judgment, her parents are letting her use her favorite shade of eyeliner—midnight blue—for the walls, but only on three conditions: She buys the paint, she does the work (and cleans up), and she repaints the room in a more, well, *traditional* shade before she leaves the nest.

Narcissa carefully hides her girlish excitement and responds by shrugging her shoulders and rolling her darkly rimmed eyes. Then she picks off a little of the black polish on the nail of her right index finger.

Her boyfriend Bruno and BFF Absinthe can help transform her ordinary room this Saturday, so Narcissa gets to work figuring out how much paint she needs to buy.

A quick web search reveals that a gallon of paint will cover about 350 square feet. But Narcissa figures she'll need to apply at least two coats, because the paint color is so dark. (Two years of art classes haven't gone to waste.) So, she'll need twice as much paint—just to be on the safe side.

Narcissa cranks up The Cure on her iPod and starts measuring. She's quick with fractions, and she finds the dimensions of her room and sketches a diagram before the last chord of "Boys Don't Cry."

And it's no wonder: Her room is basically a box—no nooks and crannies, although she'd love to live in the turret of a grand Victorian house.

The ceilings are 8 feet tall. Two walls are 14 feet wide, and the other two walls are 20 feet wide. From listening to dorky Mr. Sneft, her math teacher, she knows that to find the area of each wall, she'll just multiply the length (or, for our purposes, the height) and the width:

$$14 \cdot 8 = 112 \text{ square feet}$$
$$20 \cdot 8 = 160 \text{ square feet}$$

The mathematical abbreviation for "square feet" is ft². Narcissa knows that two walls are 112 ft² and two walls are 160 ft². That means the total square footage of the walls is

$$112 + 112 + 160 + 160 = 544 \text{ ft}^2$$

(Narcissa hasn't forgotten about the ceiling. Instead of painting it, she's decided to upholster it with a huge piece of purple velvet. The girl has ambitious plans *and* an amazing sense of style.)

How does she figure out how much paint she needs? She divides the total square footage by 350, which is the number of square feet that 1 gallon of paint is supposed to cover.

$$544 \div 350 = 1.55 \text{ gallons}$$

But remember, midnight blue will probably require two coats, so Narcissa multiplies by 2.

$$1.55 \cdot 2 = 3.1 \text{ gallons}$$

No paint store will sell her that exact amount, so Narcissa rounds up and buys 4 gallons of midnight blue paint.

But she *could* do something else. Remember, there are 4 quarts in 1 gallon. Another way to put this: 1 quart is 0.25 gallon. In this situation, she could buy 3 gallons and 1 quart, because 3.25 gallons (3 gallons + 1 quart) is larger than 3.1 gallons (the amount of paint she needs).

Now all Narcissa needs is the velvet.

Windows to the Mind

If you're looking around your living room right now, envisioning what it would look like in midnight blue, you've probably spotted something we didn't take into consideration in our above calculation:

doors and windows. Because Narcissa isn't going to paint the windows in her room (unless she's *really* into Goth) and probably not the doors, either, shouldn't she consider subtracting out the square footage of the windows and doors in order to reach a more exact calculation of how much paint she'll need? If she needs to be extra careful about her purchase, sure.

Luckily, the experts have figured out two simple rules:

Most doors are about 20 ft^2
Most standard windows are 15 ft^2

Narcissa has 4 windows and 2 doors, so she does these calculations:

Doors	$2 \cdot 20 = 40$ ft^2
Windows	$4 \cdot 15 = 60$ ft^2

So, if we add $40 + 60$, we'll see that the windows and doors take up 100 ft^2 of the room—area that she's not going to paint. So she can subtract that from the total she found earlier:

$$544 - 100 = 444 \text{ ft}^2$$

And she can divide by 350 again to find out how many gallons it will take to cover 444 square feet:

$$444 \div 350 = 1.27$$

Then she needs to multiply by 2 (for the two coats of paint):

$$1.27 \cdot 2 = 2.54$$

Length • Width

You may have noticed that Narcissa used the formula for the area of a rectangle to find the total square feet in each wall.

$$A = lw$$

A is the area of the wall

l is the length of the wall

w is the width of the wall

Then she added the areas of all the walls to find the *surface area* of her walls.

In school, you probably spent some time finding the total surface area of solids, such as prisms and pyramids. In these cases, you found the area of each side and then added them together. But sometimes you want the surface area of only some sides—like the walls of a room, but not the ceiling or floor. In this case, you only need to add the areas of the sides that you're interested in.

If you think of a room as a three-dimensional figure (specifically, a rectangular prism), it's easy to see how this would work for all types of 3-dimensional shapes.

No funny-looking glasses required.

Narcissa should be just fine with 2½ gallons of paint (in other words, 2 gallons and 2 quarts). That's quite a bit less than her original calculation!

Switching Up

When Bruno picks up Narcissa to go to the paint store, he looks at her calculations. "You did this wrong," he mutters glumly.

Narcissa grabs the paper from his gloved hand and looks again.

"No I didn't!" she hollers.

"Look," Bruno says, "I remember that Dear Aunt Sally stuff, and you've done the math in the wrong order. You have to *multiply* before you *divide*."

He grabs the paper from Narcissa's hand, fishes a stubby pencil from the front pocket of his black jeans, and scribbles down some numbers.

$$444 \text{ ft}^2$$
$$2 \text{ coats of paint}$$
$$444 \cdot 2 = 888 \text{ ft}^2$$
$$888 \div 350 =$$

He stops and scratches his long goatee with the nub of his pencil. "Huh."

Narcissa gloats. "See, I did it right," she says. "888 divided by 350 is 2.54. Hah!"

Why are both of them right? Because it doesn't matter whether you multiply first or divide first.

In other words, PEMDAS = PEDMAS (Please Excuse Dark Moods And Songs).

Remember what I said about there often being different ways to reach the same answer?

Hit the Floor

In the morning, it can be awfully tough to crawl out of bed—and when the hardwood floor is freezing, Micah dreads the thought of leaving his cocoon of blankets.

He decides it's time to put in some fluffy shag carpet, with a pile so deep that he won't be able to see his toes. Heaven!

But Micah doesn't trust those guys at Budget Carpet. Sure, their prices can't be beat, but he's certain they're making up the difference by overestimating the amount of carpet customers need. He decides to figure out how much carpet he'll need, before *they* start measuring.

In short, he needs to know the area of his floor. This would be no problem if his floor were a perfect square—or a rectangle. But it's not! He has an L-shaped room: the main part, plus an alcove.

Micah takes some measurements and draws a sketch of his room. Then, squinting, he realizes that his L-shaped room is actually 2 rectangles. That gives him an idea for how to solve his problem. All he has to do is find the area of each of these rectangles and then add them together. Violà! He measures the main part of the room. The length is 15 feet, and the width is 33 feet. He calls the area of this part of the room Area 1, or A_1:

$$A_1 = 15 \cdot 33$$
$$A_1 = 495 \text{ ft}^2$$

Next he measures the alcove, which is a square that measures 25 feet by 25 feet. He calls the area of this part of the room Area 2, or A_2:

$$A_2 = 25 \cdot 25$$
$$A_2 = 625 \text{ ft}^2$$

To figure the total amount he needs, or A, he adds together A_1 and A_2:

$$A = A_1 + A_2$$
$$A = 495 + 625$$
$$A = 1{,}120 \text{ ft}^2$$

So Micah needs 1,120 ft^2 of carpeting. What if he wants to carpet his walk-in closet, too? Then he just needs to find the area of the floor and add that to the 1,120 ft^2 he already knows he needs.

Wall to Wallet

What's the price tag of that gorgeous shag carpet that Micah wants to install? Budget Carpet has a deal for $10.99 per square yard. So he needs to do a little more math to see whether he can actually afford this luxury. His floor is 1,120 ft^2. How many square yards is that?

There are 3 feet in a yard, so the calculation is pretty simple. Just divide the number of square feet that you need by 9.

Wait! Why 9? Don't you divide by 3?

Nope. Remember, you're working with squared units. There are 3 feet in a yard, so there are 9 square feet in a square yard. (Yep, all you've done is squared 3—that is, multiplied itself by itself—to get 9.)

Micah breaks out his trusty calculator and comes up with

$$1{,}120 \div 9 = 124.44444444 \ldots$$

Because the decimal is less than ½, he should round down, right? Not so fast. When ordering materials, it's always best to round up; that way you have a little extra, just in case, instead of not enough. So it looks like Micah might want to order 125 square yards of carpet.

That means he'll pay

$$\$10.99 \cdot 125$$
$$\$1{,}373.75$$

And that doesn't include the installation fees.

Maybe buying an area rug or a nice pair of wool socks is a better plan.

Subversive Numbers

When Micah was calculating the area of his bedroom, why did he use the little number at the bottom right corner of his variables? Remember how he referred to Area 1 as A_1 and to Area 2 as A_2? That little number is called a subscript, and it's how Micah distinguished between the area of his main room and the area of his alcove. In other words,

> A_1 is the area of the main room.
> A_2 is the area of the square.
> A is the total area of the floor.

But why not use completely different letters? Why not call the area of the main room m, the area of the alcove a, and the total area T?

You certainly could. But A is useful, because it shows that all three results represent area.

(Did you figure it out on your own? Even if you didn't, give yourself an A for effort.)

Scaled to Size

Which is easier: dragging heavy furniture around a room or drawing a picture? If you're trying to find out whether that king-size bed you've got your eye on will fit in your bedroom and still let you open your closet door, a scale drawing can help you figure it out.

If you're planning a major overhaul—including paint, flooring, and new furniture—a scale drawing can help you estimate materials and prices before you even set foot in a home improvement store.

In a scale drawing, the measurements on paper are in proportion to the actual measurements. For example, your scale may be ¼" to 1'. This means that every ¼" in the drawing is equal to 1' in the room itself. (Did you know that each of the squares on graph paper is about ¼" by ¼"? That's why the ¼"-to-1' scale is really common.)

Luckily, there are some easy steps for making a ¼"-to-1' scale drawing of a room.

1. Measure your room.
2. Draw the outline of the room on your graph paper, remembering that each box represents 1'. If the length of a wall is 14½', draw a line that is 14½ boxes long.
3. Be careful to consider all irregularities of the room, such as bay windows, bump-outs, and weird angles.
4. Mark off doors and windows. Do this by measuring from the molding to an adjoining wall.
5. Label all measurements carefully.

Want to get really fancy? You can also make scale drawings of the furniture. Cut these pieces out of another piece of graph paper, and you can try them in different positions in the room—without back strain.

Fitting the Fridge

Remember, a room is three-dimensional, with 3-D components, like tables, cabinets, and the kitchen sink. And that's what makes renovating a kitchen such a difficult task. Not only do you have to think of the surfaces—floors, walls, and ceilings—but you have to think of the cabinets, countertops, and appliances. Because these are 3-D objects, you have one extra opportunity to make a mistake.

The fridge can be the most challenging appliance to measure for, because it often has cabinets on one or both sides and above it. One little error can mean not being able to open the refrigerator door or—worse—not being able to fit the darned thing in the space allotted.

This problem can arise in either of two different forms: Either you have the fridge and are building the cabinets, or you're buying a fridge for existing cabinets. Let's look at the first scenario.

Eli is renovating his kitchen, and one thing is for certain. He wants the Zero-Below side-by-side refrigerator with a pull-out freezer drawer at the bottom. In other words, he needs to make sure that the cabinets he is having installed will leave room for this particular fridge. He has the manufacturer's guidelines for the appliance: The width is 48", the height is 84", and the depth (without the door and handle) is 25". These guidelines also suggest that he leave no more than ¼" between the fridge and the cabinets or wall. What should the dimensions of this space be?

First, Eli considers the depth. He needs the fridge to be ¼" away from the wall, so he adds that to the depth of the appliance: 25" + ¼" = 25¼". Now for the height: The fridge should be ¼" from the top cabinet, but it's resting on the floor, so he only needs to add ¼" to the height: 84" + ¼" = 84¼".

The width is a little different. Because this is a built-in refrigerator, Eli needs to consider the cabinets on either side of the fridge. That means he'll add ¼" to each side: ¼" + 48" + ¼" = 48½".

Thus the space he needs for his beloved Zero-Below is 48½"×84¼"×25¼".

But Josh has a slightly different problem. After 15 years, his fridge bit the dust. He needs to replace it, but he doesn't want to change his cabinets. The space for the refrigerator is 45"×84"×24". What is the largest icebox he can buy?

Josh needs to do the opposite of what Eli did; he needs to subtract from these dimensions. The guidelines are the same: The distance between the refrigerator and the walls or cabinets should be no more than ¼".

Like Eli, Josh starts with the depth, but unlike Eli, he *subtracts* ¼" from the depth of the cabinets: 45"−¼". Doing a little mental math, he figures out that the result is 44¾". Then he moves to the height, subtracting ¼" from 84": 84"−¼"=83¾".

Again, though, the width is a little trickier. His space is 24" wide, but he has to subtract ¼" from *each side*. That means he has to subtract a total of ½": 24"−½"=23½".

Now he just needs to ask Eli to go shopping with him and help him move the new refrigerator into place.

Pretty as a Picture

Hanging pictures can be a tricky business. If you're not careful, your foyer can look like a hall of mirrors—with crooked photos of your wedding party alongside drawings that your kid made in kindergarten. Not to mention the holes in the drywall from when you realized that you hung your college diploma so high up the wall that only a giant could read it.

Not exactly the look you were going for?

You may not want to face it, but a tape measure, pencil, and yes, even a level, are your best buddies in home decorating. And hanging anything on your walls is no exception. Let's look at this in a bit more detail.

Mimsy Mimsiton is thrilled to have finally received the oil portrait of her dear Mr. Cuddles, a teacup poodle who is set to inherit her large fortune. The painting will look *fabulous* above the marble fireplace in the west-wing lounge of her mansion.

But drat! The museum curator Mimsy has on retainer is in Paris, looking for additions to Mimsy's collection of French landscapes. (She's redoing the upstairs powder room and wants just the right Monet to round out the décor.)

But the painting must be hung before Mr. Cuddles's birthday party. His little poodle friends would be so disappointed not to see it! There's no way around it; Mimsy's poor, overworked House Manager must hang the painting herself.

Luckily, House Manager is no stranger to the DIY trend, and Butler will be there to help. The two meet in the lounge, where the painting has already been delivered—along with a stepladder, a tape measure, and a pencil. Once House Manager marks the spot, Handy Man will come along to safely secure the painting to the wall.

House Manager and Butler get to work. First they measure the painting: With the gilded frame, it's 54" tall and 60" wide.

Next, they turn their attention to the space above the mantle. House Manager climbs atop the ladder, while Butler holds it steady. From the ceiling to the top of the mantle is 84". The width of the mantle is 75".

Climbing down from the ladder, House Manager notes that the painting will certainly fit in the space allotted. She knows from experience that it is to be centered over the mantle. However, Mimsy will have a fit if the painting is centered vertically—between the ceiling and the mantle. No, the bottom of the painting must be *exactly* 12" above the mantle.

So how high should Handy Man install the picture hanger?

To find out, House Manager must add 12" to 54" (the height of the painting). The top of the painting should be 66" above the mantle.

House Manager grabs her tape measure again and removes the freshly sharpened pencil from behind her ear. Then she climbs the ladder. Starting at one end of the mantle, she measures 37½"—which is half the width of the mantle. She makes a barely visible pencil mark at that point.

Then from there, she measures up the wall to 64". Again, she carefully makes a faint pencil mark.

If House Manager stopped here—leaving that small mark for Handy Man to hang the portrait—she'd probably be out of a job. That's because she's merely marked the top of the frame, not where the hanger should be secured.

She descends the ladder and goes back to the portrait. Turning it around, she notices the picture wire that has been stretched from one side to the other. She hooks her finger under the center of the wire and pulls up gently—creating an angle, as if the picture wire were hanging on a nail. Now an angle is a two-dimensional figure formed by two lines (called rays) that share a common point. Here's an easier way to remember this: An angle looks like a V.

If she can measure the distance from the top of the frame to the vertex—the point where two sides of an angle meet—she'll be in business.

There's just one more thing to consider: Is the vertex of the angle too far to the left or too far to the right? For the painting to hang straight and be centered on the mantle, the vertex must be located at exactly half the width of the portrait.

House Manager uses her tape measure to find the length of each leg of the angle. In other words, she measures the distance from one end of the picture wire to the vertex of the angle and then the distance from the vertex of the angle to the other end of the wire. If the vertex is centered properly, the legs of the angle will have the same length.

Moving her finger ever so slightly, House Manager centers the vertex of the wire angle—and measures from that point to the top of the picture frame: 9".

She now can make the final mark for Handy Man. She climbs the ladder for the third time and measures 9" from the mark she made earlier. Again, being very careful, she makes a tiny mark on the wall.

House Manager's work is done. If anything goes wrong now, it's Handy Man's fault.

She folds up the ladder and gathers her supplies. Then she's off to order beef cupcakes for Mr. Cuddles's party.

Going Wireless

You need a piece of art to cover the hole in the wall where your brother accidentally shot off his Official Red Ryder Carbine-Action Two-Hundred-Shot Range Model Air Rifle. And at a spring yard sale, you find just what you've been looking for—a black velvet Elvis, ebony-painted wood frame and all.

When you get home, you notice the problem right away. The Elvis's back has no picture wire or hook. Luckily, your mom gave you a home-improvement kit when you moved into your trailer, and even more remarkably, you know where it is.

The kit includes a length of wire, two eye screws, and a picture hanger to nail into the wall. But where the heck should you put the screws? And how long should the wire be?

The kit instructions give a little bit of direction:

1. Cut the wire so that it's 1½ times the width of the picture.
2. Install the screws ⅔ of the way from the bottom of the frame.

First, deal with the wire. At that same yard sale, you bought an old yardstick, which you use to measure the width of the frame: 30". How do you find 1½ times 30"? As always, you have some choices. You can multiply 30 by 1.5. Or, if you're up for some mental math, try this:

$$\frac{1}{2} \text{ of } 30 \text{ is } 15$$
$$30 + 15 = 45$$
$$\text{so } 1\frac{1}{2} \text{ times } 30 \text{ is } 45$$

You measure 45" of the wire and cut it.

Now you have to deal with the eye screws. You can measure ⅔ from the bottom of the frame or ⅓ from the top of the frame. Either way, you need to do some math.

The frame is 42" tall, and ⅓ of 42 is the same thing as 42 ÷ 3, or 14". Thus you can measure 14" from the top of the frame to find where you should put the eye screws.

You call your brother over to install the eye screws. (He caused the problem to begin with, and believe it or not, he's better with hand tools.) Within the hour, Elvis is on the wall.

Thank you. Thank you very much.

Good Morning, Sunshine!

Unless your nearest neighbor is in the next county, you probably want to ensure yourself some privacy by way of curtains, shades, or drapes. (And in an old house, drapes are practically a necessity—they block drafts from 100-year-old windowpanes!)

Hanging curtains is another DIY project that can make you want to pitch your cordless drill through the nearest sliding glass door. But if you take this project in small steps, you can feel like the queen or king of home improvement. You might even try building a deck!

But you're getting ahead of yourself.

As with most house projects, you'll need to take some measurements. Drawing a picture is also really helpful. And rather than guessing where you should hang the curtain rods, why not turn to some real-live decorators—or at least to their advice from books, websites, or television shows? Let's look in on someone who's doing this.

Sarah is so tired. Her precious little baby, Sine, is not so precious when he wakes up at dawn. And in the Alaska summer, dawn comes way,

way too early. If she could get just an hour more sleep each morning, she'd feel like a new person.

Time for some blackout curtains for the baby's room.

She consults a decorator friend for advice. He gives her five important pieces of information:

1. Sarah will need two panels for each of the two windows in Sine's room. That's four panels in all.

2. For fullness, the width of the curtains should be twice the width of the window, so each panel should be the same width as the window.

3. To block out the light, the curtains should hang from just above the top molding to just above the floor.

4. The curtain rod brackets should be hung 5" on either side of the molding.

5. No moose prints!

While Sine is out fishing with his dad, Sarah takes some measurements. Both windows in Sine's room are the same size. She draws a quick sketch and fills in the measurements.

- Width: 30"
- From the top of the window molding to just above the floor: 64"

Sarah is ready to order the curtains. What dimensions will she need?

Looking at her sketch and considering the advice her friend gave her, she knows she needs to buy four panels that are 30" wide by 64" tall. Because the curtain rods will need to extend 5" past the molding on each side, her two curtain rods will have to be at least 40" long (5" on the left side of the window + 30" for the window width + 5" on the left side of the window = 40").

Sarah orders the curtains and hardware and pays extra for overnight delivery. Only one more early wake-up call with Sine! She plugs in her rechargeable drill before she goes to bed that night.

The next day Sarah's package arrives, and she is ready. She's strapped her tool belt around her waist and loaded it up with everything she needs—a retractable tape measure, cordless drill, sharpened pencil, drill bits, and a Phillips screwdriver.

Her drawing shows exactly where to position her curtain rods so that the curtains will fall exactly where they should. And before Sine is ready for his afternoon nap, Sarah has his new drapes installed.

It's curtains for her early bird.

Super Problem Solver

Math in the everyday world can be challenging for one big reason: There are too many darned steps! Even people with long attention spans and great spatial abilities can get lost in a matter of moments.

Some basic problem-solving skills can help out in a pinch.

1. Make a list.
   If your head is swimming with numbers, do a brain dump. In other words, list everything you know about the problem. Then cross off what you don't need.

2. Draw a picture.
   It doesn't take a Rembrandt to whip up a sketch of a room and label its dimensions.

3. Make a table.
   Organizing the information so that it makes sense can point you to the perfect solution.

4. Look for clues.
   Certain words will tell you what you need to do: *per* means "each," *squared* means "times itself," and even little old *is* means "equals" or "is equal to."

5. Rewrite the problem.
   Sometimes you just need to write things in a different way. And—surprise!—sometimes writing an equation with variables is just the thing.

6. Check your answer.
   You don't need to call up your algebra teacher to see if your answer is right. But it is a good idea to ask yourself, "Is this answer *reasonable*?"

5

In the Kitchen: Making More, Making Less— Recipe Math to the Rescue!

Ah, the sweet smells from the kitchen! Freshly baked bread, spicy garlic and onions, ginger cookies—and the whiff of smoke coming from your ears as you attempt to halve your great-grandmother's biscuit recipe.

The kitchen is both a delight and a source of great frustration. The dozens of culinary magazines, television programs, and websites are testament to the true art and science of baking and cooking. And as you probably learned long ago, math plays a role. From adjusting recipes to converting measurements, a little bit of arithmetic can either make or break a dish.

But it's not hard! If you can scramble an egg or even make toast, you can do basic kitchen math and reap the delicious benefits day after day.

Saucy Re-Sizing

Graham has a green thumb. When he planted a few tomato plants in his backyard, he had no idea that he'd be overwhelmed with the ruby-red fruits all summer long. His neighbors and coworkers are sick of them, and so is Graham. It's time for a secret weapon: Mom's spaghetti sauce.

See, Graham figures that he can stash a big batch of red sauce in the freezer and eat well all fall and winter long. He might even have enough to share, once everyone has forgotten the mounds of tomatoes he's already given away. But first he has to figure out how to adjust the recipe.

His last tomato harvest yielded 25 tomatoes, and he'd like to use them all. But Mom's recipe calls for 10 tomatoes. Clearly, he'll need to increase the batch, but by how much? Twice? Three times? Something in between?

The answer may be clear to you. But if not, here's another way to ask this question: 25 is how many times 10? Or 10 times what is 25?

$$25 = 10 \cdot ?$$

Remember, we can substitute x for the question mark:

$$25 = 10 \cdot x$$

And we don't need the multiplication sign:

$$25 = 10x$$

Now all Graham needs to do is solve the equation. That will tell him the number by which he needs to multiply each ingredient amount in order to correctly alter the recipe.

Math by the Jar

If Graham has a bumper tomato crop, he'll want to do something else with those saucy fruits, too. And canning is just the thing. In the winter, home-canned tomatoes are perfect for chili, lasagna, or more spaghetti sauce.

Fortunately, Graham has his mother's canning recipes, as well. She says that about 7 tomatoes will fill one 1-quart jar.

Graham pokes around in his basement for some canning supplies. And he hits pay dirt—16 canning jars.

The problem is that the jars are different sizes. He brings them upstairs and puts them in groups: six 1-pint jars, eight 1-quart jars, and two 2-quart jars.

With these jars, how many tomatoes can he can?

First things first. The 2-quart jars are twice as big as the 1-quart jars. For each of those jars, Graham needs to double the number of tomatoes that can fit in a 1-quart jar.

$$2 \cdot 7 = 14 \text{ tomatoes fit in a 2-quart jar}$$

The pint jars are half the size of the quart jars. Because 7 tomatoes fit in a 1-quart jar,

$$\frac{1}{2} \cdot 7 = 3.5 \text{ tomatoes fit in a pint jar}$$

Now he can estimate the number of tomatoes for each size jar.

$$\text{six pint jars} \rightarrow 6 \cdot 3.5 = 21 \text{ tomatoes}$$
$$\text{eight quart jars} \rightarrow 8 \cdot 7 = 56 \text{ tomatoes}$$
$$\text{two 2-quart jars} \rightarrow 2 \cdot 14 = 28 \text{ tomatoes}$$

And now he can add:

$$21 + 56 + 28 = 105 \text{ tomatoes}$$

After the next heat wave, Graham should have plenty to do.

In Chapter 2, we reviewed how to isolate an unknown quantity (x), by doing the same thing to each side of the equals sign. We also reviewed the fact that the inverse of multiplication is division. Thus, to separate the x from $10x$, we need to divide both sides of the equation by 10.

$$\frac{25}{10} = \frac{10x}{10}$$

$$2.5 = x$$

This means that Graham has 2.5 times as many tomatoes as the recipe calls for. If he wants to use all of the tomatoes—and he really, really does!—he'll have to increase the amounts of all the ingredients by 2.5. In other words, he needs to multiply each ingredient amount by 2.5 before measuring.

But for all of Graham's horticultural talents, he's not big on using a calculator. He figures he can do the math in his head. And turns out he's right. Remember that 2.5 is the same thing as 2½, so all Graham needs to do is this:

1. Double the original amount.
2. Find half of the original amount.
3. Add.

Let's apply these steps to the ½ cup of olive oil that the original recipe calls for:

Double ½ cup → **1 cup**
Half of ½ cup → **¼ cup**
1 cup + ¼ cup = 1¼ cups

And what about the carrots (Mom's secret ingredient)?

Double 3 cups → 6 cups
Half of 3 cups → 1½ cups
6 cups + 1½ cups = 7½ cups

By evening, when the summer temperatures have fallen, Graham has a big pot of red sauce simmering on the stove—and not a single tomato left on his plants.

Crafty Conversions

Cooking can be an adventure, especially if your 2-year-old has taken off with your measuring cups. Or what if you need 2 cups of whipping cream, which is sold only in pints or quarts?

That's where a simple conversion chart can come in handy. Whether you're adjusting a recipe or making do with limited tools, knowing a few conversions makes life in the kitchen much easier.

⅛ teaspoon or less = a pinch
3 teaspoons = 1 tablespoon
4 tablespoons = ¼ cup
5⅓ tablespoons = ⅓ cup
8 tablespoons = ½ cup
10⅔ tablespoons = ⅔ cup
16 tablespoons = 1 cup
2 cups = 1 pint
4 cups = 1 quart
2 pints = 1 quart
4 quarts = 1 gallon

Getting Improper

Some fractions can be written two ways. The amount of olive oil that Graham needs in his altered version of Mom's spaghetti sauce recipe is 1¼ cups. That's a mixed number: It has a whole number (the 1) and a fraction (the ¼).

But that number can also be written entirely as a fraction. 1 cup is the same as ⁴⁄₄, right? (Imagine a pie cut into fourths. If you keep them all, you're keeping the whole pie.) So ⁴⁄₄ plus ¼ is ⁵⁄₄. When you add fractions that have the same denominator (the bottom number), you just add the numerators (the top numbers) together and keep the denominator the same. So, ¼ is the same as ⁵⁄₄.

A fraction in which the numerator is larger than the denominator is called an improper fraction. If you have a mixed number such as 2¼, where the whole number is larger than 1, there's another way to change a mixed number to an improper fraction.

First, multiply the whole number by the denominator of the fraction:

$$2¼ \rightarrow 2 \cdot 4 = 8$$

Then add that number to the numerator of the mixed number:

$$8 + 1 = 9$$

That number becomes the numerator of the improper fraction:

$$\frac{9}{?}$$

But what is the denominator? It's the same as the denominator in the mixed number:

$$\frac{9}{4}$$

So, 2¼ = 9⁄4.

Suppose Graham knows that he needs 5⁄4 cup of olive oil, but he doesn't want to measure out ¼ cup five times. He can convert that improper fraction to a mixed number. He should just divide the numerator by the denominator (the top number by the bottom one): 5 ÷ 4 = 1. That 1 is the whole number. But there's a 1 left over also, right? That's the remainder. Pop that remainder on top of the original denominator (which was 4), and you end up with ¼. Add them together and you get 1¼ cups.

Why would you need to use improper fractions? Let's say you need 2½ cups of flour, but you have only a ½-cup measure. How many times do you need to dip your ½-cup measure into the flour canister to get 2½ cups? Think of 2½ cups as an improper fraction:

2 (the whole number) • 2 (the denominator) = 4 + 1 (the numerator) = 5⁄2 (put the new number over the old denominator)

That's 5 half-cups of flour.

Part by Part

Have you ever wondered how the chefs in television contests come up with such delicious dishes—without a recipe? Well, they're masters of their craft, of course, but they also depend on some basic formulas, many of which are shown as ratios.

A ratio is a way of showing the relationship between two numbers. In Chapter 4, we talked about scale drawings, and we said that often in such drawings, ¼" = 1'. That's a ratio. Every ¼" on the drawing corresponds to 1' in the real world. Because ratios are usually written with a colon, we could have represented this ratio as 1': ¼".

We often use the word *part* when we're talking about ratios. That's because we use ratios to show the relationship between different things. For example, Joe likes a stiff drink after work each day. If he mixes three ounces of Scotch with one ounce of water, the ratio is 3:1.

Here's another example. Felice finally has her own place in the Big Apple. She plunked down a crazy amount of cash for her studio apartment, which means she'll be on a tight budget from now to eternity.

But that's okay with her. If she can make it here, she can make it anywhere.

Felice has a futon, which does double duty as both bed and couch. Her grandmother gave her a card table and four folding chairs. And she picked up a pot, a skillet, and a set of mismatched dishes at a flea market in The Village. The can opener and a handful of flatware were left behind by a former roommate.

In other words, she's all set, as long as she doesn't need to make any fancy meals. For now, she'll live on leftover pizza, salads, and canned soup.

But these menus get old quickly. Before she knows it, Felice is ready for something different. She can't afford to buy any specialty cooking tools—not even a measuring cup—and she still needs to eat on the cheap.

Long-grain white rice is a great option. It's versatile, and she can make it with everything she has on hand. Her grandmother not only gave her a place to eat but also taught her how to make rice—using a 2:1 ratio, or 2 parts water to 1 part rice.

That means Felice can use a regular coffee mug to measure her rice and water. It doesn't matter how big the coffee mug is, as long as she keeps the ratio the same. She fills her mug with rice and pours it into the pot. Then, using the same mug, she adds 2 mugs of water. She brings it all to a boil, turns down the heat, and covers it with the lid. In 15 to 20 minutes, she has fluffy white rice to serve with sautéed veggies.

Yum!

But what if she wants to entertain? Changing a ratio is simple. To double the recipe, she merely doubles each part: 4 parts water to 2 parts rice. And what if one day she isn't as hungry as usual? She can simply reduce the ratio: 1 part water to ½ part rice.

Here's hoping that rice doesn't get too old too soon.

Revealing Ratios

A ratio is just a way to show the relationship between numbers. Mathematically speaking, ratios compare only two numbers.

Ratios can be written in the following three different ways.

- 2:1
- $\frac{2}{1}$
- 2 to 1

Ratios can also be written as fractions, which means they can also be written as percents.

All you need to do is divide the denominator into the numerator and change the answer to a percent, like this:

$$3:4 = \frac{3}{4}$$
$$3 \div 4 = 0.75$$
$$0.75 = 75\%$$

In other words, ratios are more flexible than the most adept chef or baker. Despite the fact that, mathematically speaking, a ratio shows the relationship between two numbers, in the kitchen, cooks may use more complex "ratios" with more than two numbers.

Technically, these aren't real ratios because they can't be written as fractions or percents, but they do show the relationships among ingredients. For example, the typical ratio for baking biscuits is 3:2:1— that is, 3 parts flour, 2 parts liquid, 1 part fat. How does this work in the kitchen?

If you had 3 cups of flour, you would need 2 cups of liquid and 1 cup of fat. But what if you had 6 cups of flour? Well, $6 = 2 \cdot 3$, so you would need to multiply each of your other numbers in the "ratio" by 2.

$$2 \cdot 2 = 4$$
$$1 \cdot 2 = 2$$

You would need 4 cups of liquid and 2 cups of fat.

And of course you can reduce a recipe this way, too. If you had 1 cup of flour, you would need to reduce the other ingredients by ⅓. (That's because 3 = 6 ÷ 3, or 6 • ⅓.) To find out how much of the other ingredients you need, just multiply by ⅓.

$$2 \bullet \tfrac{1}{3} = \tfrac{2}{3}$$
$$1 \bullet \tfrac{1}{3} = \tfrac{1}{3}$$

So you would need ⅔ cup of liquid and ⅓ cup of fat.

Talking Turkey

As any experienced cook will tell you, timing is often the most difficult skill to master in the kitchen. Nobody wants to sit down to a meal of overdone fish, cold broccoli, and room-temperature biscuits. (The butter should melt into the flaky layers, you know?)

Figuring out how long a dish should bake, roast, or boil is the first step to presenting a carefully choreographed dinner. And for many novice or not-so-frequent home chefs, a giant turkey is the most daunting of all entrées.

Sure, you can count on the pop-up timer. These come with some turkeys, or you can buy one separately. But you'll still need to know when to put the bird in the oven—and when to start boiling the potatoes.

And there's also the thawing time. Buying a frozen turkey means allowing time for it to defrost, which is probably a lot longer than you think!

But you don't need Julia Child or a semester at Le Cordon Bleu to figure any of this out. Thawing times and cooking times depend on the turkey's weight.

It's your first Thanksgiving with your new husband, Tom. And your mother-in-law will arrive just in time for the 6:00 P.M. dinner. She's bringing pecan pie, stuffing, and homemade rolls. You're in charge of all the rest—including the turkey. You've ordered a 12-pound bird, which you'll need to thaw in the fridge before roasting. When should you pull it out of the deep freeze?

You know from your sister's horror stories that you can't cut corners by thawing the bird on the counter. Unless you want to host the Thanksgiving-dinner-when-everyone-got-*Salmonella*, your best bet is to defrost the turkey in the refrigerator. The United States Department of Agriculture (USDA) says to allow 5 hours of thawing time per pound. They oughta know, right?

You've bought a 12-pound turkey. How long should you allow for thawing?

It's a simple problem, really. Just multiply the number of pounds by 5—the number of hours needed to thaw each pound.

$$12 \cdot 5 = 60$$

So, you need to put the turkey in the fridge for 60 hours in order to thaw it. But let's think a moment. Does this mean 60 hours before dinner is served? Nope. The USDA also says that serving raw poultry is a big no-no, so you'll also need to roast the bird.

If your oven is set to 325°F, the USDA recommends roasting an unstuffed turkey for 2¾ to 3 hours. They're the experts on avoiding food-borne illnesses, so you decide to follow their recommendations.

With a little time for resting—the turkey, not you—and carving, you estimate that it will take 3 to 3¼ hours to get the bird from the fridge to the table. You'll need to add that to the thawing time in order to figure out when to pull the turkey out of the freezer.

$$60 + 3¼ = 63¼ \text{ hours}$$

Clearly you'll need more than a day, but how much more? There are 24 hours in a day. How many 24s are there in 63¼? You can use a calculator, but that could be confusing. Instead, try some mental math.

To make things easier, forget about the extra ¼ hour (or 15 minutes). You can add that on to the end. Working with whole numbers is much easier.

It looks like you'll need at least 2 days. That's because 24 times 2 is 48, which is less than the total time you have figured out. Will you need a third day? You can subtract to find out.

$$63 - 48 = 15$$

So, 2 days and 15 hours (plus the extra 15 minutes) ought to do it. But that doesn't tell you *what time* to start defrosting the turkey, does it?

Remember, your dinner starts at 6:00 P.M. Fifteen hours before that is 3:00 A.M., and another 15 minutes before *that* is 2:45 A.M. So you will have to take the turkey out of the freezer at 2:45 A.M. on the Tuesday before Thanksgiving.

Because you're doing all the cooking, you decide to let Tom get up to move the turkey from the freezer to the fridge. You set his alarm on Monday night and settle in for the last good night's sleep of the week.

Time on Your Side

Why is it so difficult to subtract and add time? The answer is simple. While the decimal system of numbers is based on 10s (it is also known to math geeks as a base-10 system), time is based on 60s. In other words, there are 60 seconds in a minute and 60 minutes in an hour.

But it gets even worse. The number of hours in a day is 24, which is neither base-10 nor base-60.

There is an easy fix, though. Instead of thinking of minutes, hours, and days as numbers, imagine them on a clock face. If you think of the clock face as a circle divided into 12 wedges, you can visually subtract and add time without much effort.

Take it one step further, and it's even easier. The diameter of the circle splits it into two halves—six hours on one side and six hours on the other side. That means that numbers directly across from each other on the clock are exactly six hours apart.

Because 9 is across from 3, 9:00 P.M. is six hours later than 3:00 P.M. And because 11 is across from 5, 11:00 A.M. is six hours before 5:00 A.M.

Once you can see the six-hour increments, it's not too difficult to do more challenging subtraction and addition problems. For example, 8:00 P.M. to 3:00 A.M. is 6 hours plus 1 hour, or 7 hours.

On the Side

There's no need to reinvent the Thanksgiving dinner. If you're not sure how much to buy for your dinner, consider these guidelines:

- A 1-pound bag of carrots makes 4 to 5 servings.
- A 12-ounce package of fresh cranberries makes about 2¼ cups of sauce.
- A serving of gravy is about ⅓ cup.
- 1½ pounds of fresh green beans makes 6 to 8 servings.
- A 5-pound bag of potatoes makes 10 to 12 servings.
- A 14-ounce bag of stuffing makes about 11 servings.

And then there's the almighty turkey. If you want leftovers, shoot for 1½ pounds per person. (Remember that the total weight includes bones, so you won't be serving that much to everyone.) To do the math, multiply the number of guests by 1.5.

> 8 people • 1.5 pounds = 12-pound turkey
> 10 people • 1.5 pounds = 15-pound turkey
> 12 people • 1.5 pounds = 18-pound turkey
> 14 people • 1.5 pounds = 21-pound turkey

Is it just you and your cat? Why not order Chinese?

How Variables Are Like Pets (No, Really!)

You can think of variables as the cats and dogs of the math world. Independent variables are the cats. They can get along just fine without others; they just need to have fresh bowls of water and food and a clean litter box.

But dependent variables are more like man's best friend. Except for gnawing on your grandmother's sofa, dogs can't do much of anything on their own. Hunting for food? Nope. Cleaning up after themselves? No way. Surviving the loneliness when you leave the room for even a moment? Heaven forbid! In short, their happiness depends on you, you, you.

Dependent variables are the same way. Take the turkey example. The thawing time *depends on* the weight of the turkey. A larger turkey takes longer to thaw. A smaller turkey takes less time to thaw. So the time it takes a turkey to thaw is a dependent variable.

But the weight of the turkey is independent. You can buy a bird of whatever size you want. Be a rebel! Go for individual Cornish game hens. Or get a huge turkey so you can have plenty of leftovers. Think like your cat and do what makes you happy—independent of the whims and wishes of your friends and family.

But whatever you do, save some for the dog. Remember, she depends on you.

Too Darned Hot

It's the chance of her culinary lifetime. Gina has been invited to Paris to compete in a worldwide bake-off. She's booked her flight, packed her supplies, and carefully adjusted her pecan-surprise toffee recipe to European-friendly metric units. To ensure absolute freshness, she will shell the pecans just hours before she's expected to make her candies, and black strap molasses is being flown in from the Caribbean.

What could go wrong?

After enjoying a leisurely breakfast on her hotel room balcony, Gina strolls to the contest kitchen to get started. That's when it hits her: She forgot her candy thermometer.

See, the trick to good toffee is cooking the molasses to the right temperature—307°F, to be exact. Without her thermometer, Gina has no chance.

But on her counter is the answer to her quickly muttered prayers. Along with a collection of spatulas, whisks, and measuring utensils is a shiny new candy thermometer.

Gina almost relaxes until she notices something odd. The thermometer only measures up to 200°. She's in Paris, where temperatures are measured in the Celsius, not the Fahrenheit, temperature scale.

She'll have to do some math to make this work.

Luckily, Gina has the conversion formula written in her *Welcome to Paris!* guidebook, which is helpfully tucked into her bag. In the conversion formula, C = degrees Celsius, and F = degrees Fahrenheit.

$$C = \left(F - 32\right) \cdot \frac{5}{9}$$

She needs the molasses to reach 307°F, so she substitutes and then does the calculations.

$$C = \left(307 - 32\right) \cdot \frac{5}{9}$$

$$C = 275 \cdot \frac{5}{9}$$

Gina scratches her head. She needs to remember how to multiply a whole number by a fraction. After a minute, she's got it. All she needs to do is multiply the whole number by the numerator of the fraction.

$$C = \frac{275 \cdot 5}{9}$$

$$C = \frac{1375}{9}$$

She wants a decimal, rather than a fraction, so she divides.

$C = 152.777\ldots$, or 152.8

Feeling as though she narrowly missed a major kitchen catastrophe, Gina regains her composure in time to slice, simmer, and stir her way to victory.

Sweetening the Pot

It's said that baking is a science, while cooking is an art. But actually, there's a little of both in each venture. And both come in handy when you want to make changes in a recipe.

Increasing or decreasing a recipe's yield (the amount it makes) is just a matter of multiplication or division. But substituting ingredients may take a little more thought. You can even develop your own recipes based on old favorites—if you know some basic fraction arithmetic.

Betty loves chocolate chip cookies. She's used the same recipe for years and years, and now she's looking for something a little different. After a trip to Hawaii for her 50th birthday, she's inspired by the tropical flavors she tasted there—coconut and macadamia nuts, in particular.

At home once again, she pulls out her tried-and-true cookie recipe. The basic ingredients will have to stay the same, but she could substitute something for the chocolate chips. What if she used white chocolate chips, shredded coconut, and chopped macadamia nuts?

Her mouth waters, and she swears she can hear the faint strumming of a ukulele.

Betty's recipe calls for 2 cups of chocolate chips. Her plan is to replace the chocolate chips with the three tropical-inspired ingredients. But if she uses 2 cups of white chocolate chips, 2 cups of shredded coconut, *and* 2 cups of macadamia nuts, the cookie dough won't stay together. Nope, she'll have to stick with 2 cups total.

She gets out her pencil to do a little math. She has three ingredients that need to be divided so that they total 2 cups. She scribbles in the margin of her cookbook

$$2 \div 3 \rightarrow \frac{2}{3}$$

That means she should add ⅔ cup of each new ingredient (instead of the chocolate chips).

But Betty doesn't trust her 50-year-old brain. This looks right, but is it? She can find out with some simple addition.

⅔ cup of white chocolate chips
⅔ cup of shredded coconut
⅔ cup of chopped macadamia nuts
⅔ + ⅔ + ⅔ = ?

She remembers that as long as the denominators are the same, you can add fractions by adding just the numerators:

$$\frac{2}{3} + \frac{2}{3} + \frac{2}{3} = \frac{6}{3}$$

$$\frac{6}{3} = 2$$

She's done it! But wait, as much as she loves macadamia nuts, she loves coconut even more. What if she altered the ratios a little bit—for less macadamia flavor and more coconut flavor?

Betty thinks again. She could double the amount of coconut and halve the amount of macadamia nuts.

Double ⅔ cup of coconut → 4/3 cup, or 1⅓ cup
Halve ⅔ cup of macadamia nuts → 2/6 cup, or ⅓ cup

So Betty now figures she can use the following ingredients:

⅔ cup white chocolate chips

1⅓ cup coconut

⅓ cup macadamia nuts

Still not trusting herself, she decides to check her work.

$$\frac{2}{3} + \frac{4}{3} + \frac{1}{3} = \frac{7}{3}$$

Good thing she did, because ⁷⁄₄ = 2⅓. Her measurements are off by ⅓. She looks carefully at the numbers and notices something. In order to have a total of 2 cups, she needs the numerators to add up to 6 (as long as she keeps the denominators the same).

$$\frac{?}{3} + \frac{?}{3} + \frac{?}{3} = \frac{6}{3}$$

What if she used ⁴⁄₃ cups coconut and ⅓ cup macadamia nuts? How many cups of white chocolate chips would she need?

$$\frac{?}{3} + \frac{4}{3} + \frac{1}{3} = \frac{6}{3}$$

She subtracts the numerators she has from the total she needs: $6 - 4 - 1 = 1$. That gives her the answer, the number that goes in place of "?" in the previous equation.

$$\frac{1}{3} + \frac{4}{3} + \frac{1}{3} = \frac{6}{3}$$

Sweet success! She needs ⅓ cup white chocolate chips.

"That settles it," Betty says to her cat, Cookie, as she retrieves her ⅓-cup measure from the cabinet. Soon the exotic smells of the islands transport her back to the beaches of Maui.

It's almost like she's still on vacation. Except for the sink full of dirty dishes.

Cooking with ⅓s and ½s

It's not always easy to tell which fractions are larger and which are smaller. That's because it's difficult to compare fractions with different denominators. You know that ¼ cup is smaller than ¾ cup, because you're comparing like denominators. Just look at the numerator and see which is larger and which is smaller. But is ⅔ a cup larger or smaller than ¾ cup?

Here, the denominators are not the same. Can you convert them so that they are the same?

Yes! The simple thing to do is to multiple one denominator by the other denominator to get a common denominator. So if you multiply 3 • 4, you'll get 12. But because you changed the denominator, you also have to change the numerator by a corresponding amount. Here's how. For the ⅔ cup, you would have to multiply the denominator by 4 to get 12. So you multiply the numerator by the same number (4), and that keeps the ratio (remember ratios?) the same. Thus ⅔ cup = 8/12 cup.

You're not quite done. For the ¾ cup, you have to do a similar operation. To get the common denominator of 12, you have to multiply the denominator of 4 by 3. So far, so good. But now you have to multiply the numerator, too: 3 • 3 = 9. So ¾ cup = 9/12. If you compare 8/12 with 9/12, you'll see that ¾ cup is slightly larger than ⅔ cup.

But what if you have more than two fractions with different denominators?

Suppose you're making a cookie recipe that calls for ½ cup macadamia nuts, ⅔ cup milk chocolate chips, and ¾ cup raisins. But you love dark chocolate, so you are going to replace all of those ingredients with dark chocolate chunks. How do you figure out the amount of dark chocolate chunks you'll need? You'll have to add ½ cup, ⅔ cup, and ¾ cup. Now, you could multiply all those denominators together (2 • 3 • 4) to get a common denominator that will work for all of them. But that would give you a huge number you'd have to simplify. Another way to find your answer is this:

1. Find the smallest number that all of the denominators will divide into evenly. This is called the least common denominator, or LCD. (In the example above, 2, 3, and 4 all divide evenly into 12.)

2. Working with each fraction individually, divide this number by the denominator of the fraction. (In the first fraction of the example above, $12 \div 2 = 6$.)

3. Then multiply the numerator by that answer. (Because $1 \cdot 6 = 6$, ½ becomes ⁶⁄₁₂.)

4. Continue doing the same with the remaining fractions on the list.

5. Then add the numerators together and simplify (if needed) to get your answer.

In our example, the fractions become ⁶⁄₁₂, ⁸⁄₁₂, and ⁹⁄₁₂. Adding their numerators together gives us an answer of ²³⁄₁₂. If you divide 23 by 12, you'll end up with 2¹¹⁄₁₂ cups.

You look through the measuring cups in your cupboard and discover that you don't have a ¹⁄₁₂-cup measure. You look at the handy conversion chart (see the sidebar titled "Crafty Conversions"), and you discover that 16 tablespoons equals 1 cup. So how many tablespoons does ¹⁄₁₂ cup equal?

Because 1 cup equals 16 tablespoons, you can multiply ¹⁄₁₂ cup by 16 to find your answer.

$$\frac{1}{12} \cdot 16 = \frac{16}{12} = 1.333\ldots$$

You'll need 1⅓ tablespoons.

Now, suppose you're rummaging in your cupboards, and you notice you have leftover pistachios! You love love love pistachios, so you want to include them in the recipe. That means you have to decrease the dark chocolate chunks by whatever amount of pistachios you have.

You chop and measure, getting ⅓ cup pistachios. You know you need 2¹¹⁄₁₂ cups of dark chocolate chunks to substitute for the other ingredients you like less well. So you have to subtract the ⅓ cup pistachios from the

2¹⁄₁₂ cup total to find the new amount of dark chocolate chunks to add to the batter. Just as in adding fractions, to subtract fractions you have to find a common denominator. Then you subtract the numerators and you're set. (Here we go!)

First, change 2¹⁄₁₂ to an improper fraction. That will make it easier to subtract.

$$2\frac{1}{12} = \frac{25}{12}$$

Then set up the subtraction problem.

$$\frac{25}{12} - \frac{1}{3}$$

The common denominator is 12, because it's the smallest number that both 12 and 3 divide into evenly. That means the first fraction will stay the same. To find the second fraction, multiply both the numerator and the denominator by 4.

$$\frac{25}{12} - \frac{4}{12}$$

Now subtract! (Just subtract the numerators. Just as in adding, the denominator stays the same.)

$$\frac{21}{12}$$

Want to know what this is as a mixed number? Change it! 12 goes into 21 one time with 9 left over.

$$1\frac{9}{12}$$

And now you can simplify your fraction by dividing the numerator and denominator by 3.

$$1\frac{3}{4}$$

You'll need 1¾ cups of dark chocolate to go with your ⅓ cup of pistachios.

Whew! Those pistachios had better be worth it. That was a lot of work!

Bigger or Smaller—By a Fraction

When you alter a recipe, you often find yourself having to multiply or divide fractions. Here's a quick refresher.

To multiply fractions, just multiply the numerators together and then multiply the denominators. If you want to halve the amount of olive oil you need in Mom's spaghetti sauce, multiply the ¼ cup by ½:

$$1 \cdot 1 \text{ (the numerators)} = 1 \text{ and } 4 \cdot 2 \text{ (the denominators)} = 8.$$
$$¼ \cdot ½ = ⅛$$

To halve the recipe, then, you need to use ⅛ cup olive oil.

Dividing fractions is like multiplying, but you have to do one step first: Invert the second fraction. Say you have a punch recipe that serves 100 people, but you need to make a much smaller batch—reducing it to ⅑ its original size. If the original recipe calls for ¾ gallon of orange juice, how much would you need for your smaller batch?

In this case, you want to divide ¾ by 9.

$$\frac{3}{4} \div 9 = \frac{3}{4} \div \frac{9}{1}$$

First invert the second fraction—that is, turn it upside down. Then multiply.

$$\frac{3}{4} \cdot \frac{1}{9}$$

You already know that to multiply fractions, you just multiply the numerators and then the denominators.

$$3 \cdot 1 = 3 \text{ and } 4 \cdot 9 = 36$$

$$\frac{3}{4} \cdot \frac{1}{9} = \frac{3}{36} \text{ or } \frac{1}{12}$$

So, you'll need ¹⁄₁₂ gallon of orange juice for your smaller batch of punch.

And now you can alter any recipe you know!

6

In the Yard: If a Train Leaves Omaha at 8 A.M., How Much Lawn Edging Do You Need?

You may like the idea of a well-landscaped yard with room for entertaining and for the kids to play. Fresh flowers from a cutting garden look great on the dining room table, and how about cooking with herbs from your own backyard!

You can almost hear the bees buzzing in agreement. This is a wonderful plan.

But if you can't really afford the services of a landscape architect, horticulturist, or gardener, you'll be doing much of this work yourself. And you will probably require a donation of blood, sweat, and brain cells—and a little bit of help from your good friend, mathematics.

Bloomin' Flowers

If you have a yard at all, you've probably considered digging up part of the lawn and installing a flowerbed or two. Whether you fill them with multicolored blossoms or evergreens, the first step is to define the shape of those flowerbeds.

Addison's yard looks great—except for that giant dead spot in the back left corner. The neighbor's live oak shades the area so densely that grass won't grow. But Addison's been reading up on shade-loving plants. She figures a little flowerbed of hostas and impatiens will work great there.

Heading out to the backyard, Addison decides to define the space with a garden hose before she starts digging. This will give her some idea of the quantity of materials she needs to buy.

The flowerbed is in the corner, at the angle where two fences meet. She decides on a wedge shape (think of a slice of pizza), so the flowerbed will have two straight sides, where the fences are. But the third side, she decides, will be curved (also like the slice of pizza). That's pretty.

Addison whips out her measuring tape. She jots down the measurements as she goes. One straight side is 3' 10" long. The other is 3' even.

The straight sides are easy. But what about that curve? Addison decides to leave that until later; first, she needs to think about what she has to buy.

She knows that the garden center can help her figure out how many flowers she needs, so that's not a problem. But she also knows, from experience, that weeds will take over her flowerbed if she's not careful. Therefore, she decides that she needs to buy a barrier—a product known as weed guard—to put down before the topsoil and mulch. Her neighbor has offered to give her his leftover topsoil and mulch, so that's taken care of. But because she wants to keep the grass from creeping into the bed, landscape edging is a must.

Addison needs to know how much weed guard and landscape edging to buy. That, of course, depends on the size of the flower bed. If she buys too little weed guard, she won't be able to cover the entire bed. If she buys too much border, she'll have wasted her money.

But will one measurement tell her how much weed guard and landscape edging to buy? The weed guard will cover the entire flowerbed. The border will go around it. In other words, she needs enough weed guard to cover the entire *area* of the flowerbed, whereas she needs enough landscape edging to go around the entire *perimeter* of the flowerbed (that is, the distance all the way around it). Looks like she will have to make two different measurements.

Perimeter Parameters

Addison starts by figuring out the perimeter. As long as she measures all the way around the flowerbed, she'll know how much landscape edging she needs. No fancy formula involved!

To find the perimeter of her flowerbed, she can simply add together the lengths of all sides—including the curve. To measure the curve, she lays her garden hose around it and then marks on the hose, with a crayon, where the curve begins and where it ends. Then she straightens out the hose and measures between the lines she marked. (Again, nothing fancy: Straightening out the curve doesn't change the measurements.) The curved edge measures 5'. She then just adds all the sides together:

$$3'\ 10" + 3' + 5' = 11'\ 10"$$

Addison rounds up and sees she needs 12' of plastic border.

Oddly Shaped Areas

Now she just needs to figure out the area of the flowerbed. If she were dealing with a rectangle, she'd just multiply the length by the width. But Addison doesn't have a rectangle. She's going to have to get creative.

To be honest, Addison doesn't need to know the *exact* area. If she has a little too much weed barrier, that's no big deal. But having too little would be a problem. And she also doesn't want to buy double the amount she needs.

But what's the easiest way to estimate the area? She needs a familiar shape that is a little larger than her flowerbed.

Passing by her sketch, her son Mario asks, "Mommy, why are you making a triangle flowerbed?"

A light bulb goes on over Addison's head. Her flowerbed is not a triangle, of course, but it *looks* like one—at least to 4-year-old Mario. She doesn't remember the formula for the area of a triangle, but that would be easy to find out, right?

She looks at her sketch again. If she somehow straightened the curve of her flowerbed, she could make a triangle. Experimenting, she realizes that if she extends the straight lines of her wedge a bit, then she can connect them with a straight line to make a triangle that is slightly bigger than her flowerbed. If she uses that measure, she'll have some leftover weed guard, but that's better than not having enough.

Addison goes back out to the garden and moves the garden hose so that it's a straight line, with each end of the line meeting one of the fences. Now she has a perfect triangle. She measures the new line. It's 6' long.

Now it's time for some more math. What is the formula for the area of a triangle? Addison knows just the person to ask for help: her 14-year-old daughter, Grace.

"Duh," Grace says, rolling her eyes. "The area of a triangle is one-half of the base times height." And she turns back to her cell phone to finish the text she was writing when she was so *rudely* interrupted.

Addison looks at her sketch again. She knows the base of the triangle is 6', but what is the height? It's tempting to just measure one of the sides, but Addison has the nagging feeling that's not right. Looking at her sketch again, she realizes she needs to measure from the top of the triangle (the vertex opposite the base) to the base. Back out in the yard, Addison measures the height of the triangle-shaped flowerbed: 4'.

Now Addison can find the area. She just does what Grace told her. She takes half of the base of the triangle and multiplies that by the triangle's height.

$$\frac{1}{2} \cdot 6 \text{ feet} \cdot 4 \text{ feet}$$
$$3 \text{ feet} \cdot 4 \text{ feet}$$
$$12 \text{ square feet}$$

Because the answer is the area of the triangle, she uses *square feet* as her unit. The area of the triangle is 12 ft².

Now Addison knows that she needs to buy 12 ft of plastic border and 12 ft² of weed guard.

If only she could get Mario and Grace to do the digging for her.

To Estimate or Not to Estimate That Is the Question

All through your math education, you were taught precise ways to solve problems. And you may have come away from that experience thinking that math depends on that degree of precision.

Sure, math is an exact science, but *you* get to decide when you need a precise answer and when an estimate will do. The key is *thoughtful* estimation. Make sure that you're not cutting so many corners—so to speak—that you end up with an estimate that is either too small or too large.

And when you get your solution, ask yourself this question: Is it reasonable?

CHAPTER 6

Making Like Michelangelo

Addison doesn't need to be an artist to solve her flowerbed problem. But it does help that she can visualize the situation and draw a sketch.

And then there's that organization thing again. Updating her sketch and being careful with her measurements helped her be certain not to omit any of the steps in solving the problem—and to perform them in the right order.

Note that Addison didn't really know how to solve her problem at first. She created a plan while she was doing it. And this is the sign of a confident problem solver. She didn't wig out when she was unsure of something. She didn't question her abilities. She simply plodded along—using what she knew and asking someone else when she didn't know.

Having smart kids was a plus, too. (We should all be so lucky.)

Planting on the Porch

You don't have a yard, you say? But the thought of fresh tomatoes makes your mouth water? And your green thumb has been itching to create some horticultural magic?

Try container gardening!

Along with water and sunshine, all you need is a container, soil, and plants, and you're good to go.

Let's say you have four containers that are shaped like rectangular prisms (in other words, they are solid or three-dimensional rectangles). You'd like to grow four different varieties of tomato plants—one per container. How much potting soil will you need?

First, you should measure the pots. Because they are rectangular prisms, each has height, width, and length. Using a tape measure, you get these results:

Height = 20 inches
Width = 15 inches
Length = 15 inches

126

The potting soil will go *inside* the pots, of course. So you need to know the volume—how much the container will contain. The volume of a rectangular prism is length times width times height, so you multiply:

$$20 \text{ in.} \cdot 15 \text{ in.} \cdot 15 \text{ in.}$$
$$4{,}500 \text{ in}^3$$

Wait! What's that in^3 all about? Remember how you indicated square feet (ft^2) when you calculated the area of an object? Well, volume is measured in cubed amounts. Therefore, you'll need 4,500 cubic inches of potting soil. But there's a problem: The gardening center sells bags of potting soil measured in cubic *feet*, so you'll need to convert.

You have *cubic inches* and you want *cubic feet*. There are 12 inches in a foot, but how many cubic inches are there in a cubic foot?

Turns out the answer is pretty simple—and pretty intuitive.

$$1 \text{ ft}^3 = 12^3 \text{ in}^3$$

In other words, 1 cubic foot equals $12 \cdot 12 \cdot 12$ in^3, or 1,728 in^3. So, to find out how many cubic feet there are in 4,500 cubic inches, just divide.

$$4{,}500 \text{ in}^3 \div 1{,}728 \text{ in}^3 = 2.6 \text{ ft}^3$$

Okay, so you need to buy 2.6 ft^3 of potting soil—for one pot. But you have four containers to fill, so you'll need to multiply.

$$2.6 \cdot 4 = 10.4 \text{ ft}^3$$

At the garden center, you find a brand that is sold in 1.5-ft^3 bags. Arggh!!! How many bags will you need? Back to division!

$$10.4 \div 1.5 = 6.9333 \ldots$$

You can't buy 6.93333 . . . bags of potting soil, so you should round up to 7 bags.

That wasn't so bad, was it? Want to share your tomatoes?

Shape Shifters

What if you had containers with circular bases, instead of rectangular containers? The process is the same, but you'll have to use a different formula for volume.

That's because a container with a circular base is probably a cylinder. The formula for the volume of a cylinder is

$$V = \pi r^2 h$$
$$\pi = 3.14 \ldots$$

r is the radius of the base

h is the height of the cylinder

Now π (pronounced "pi") is a very important number. Mathematically speaking, it's the ratio of the circumference of a circle to its diameter—but you don't need to remember that. It's enough to know that π is a very long number that rounds to 3.14.

Finding the height is pretty easy; just measure from the bottom of the container to the top. But how do you find the radius?

The radius is half the width of the circle (half of the diameter, in other words). Instead of trying to find the center of the base of the container, just measure the base from one side to the other—as close to the center of the circle as possible—and divide by 2.

Then you can plug everything into the formula to find the volume.

What if you had a cylinder-shaped container that was 3 feet tall and had a base 2 feet wide? How much potting soil would you need? The height is 3 feet, and you need to divide the width of the base by 2 to find the radius $(2 \div 2 = 1)$.

Now you can use the formula.

$$V = \pi r^2 h$$
$$V = 3.14 \cdot 1^2 \cdot 3$$

Remembering your order of operations, you know you should handle the exponent first. (Which is super-easy in this case, because 1^2 is 1!)

$$V = 3.14 \cdot 1 \cdot 3$$

Now multiply:

$$V = 9.42 \text{ ft}^3$$

You'll need 9.42 ft^3 of potting soil for this container.

What's Your Unit?

Units of measure are a big deal when you apply math to everyday situations. Here are some basics to keep in mind:

When you're measuring volume, you'll get a cubed unit. That's because you're measuring the space inside a three-dimensional figure. Get it? Three-dimensional → unit^3.

When you're measuring area, you'll get a squared unit. That's because you're measuring the space inside a two-dimensionl figure (a plane). Two-dimensional → unit^2.

And when you're measuring length, you'll get a plain old unit. That's because you're measuring a one-dimensional figure (a line). One-dimensional → unit^1, or unit.

But what about the surface area of a three-dimensional figure? Is that measured in cubic units? Nope. Because you're measuring area, it's still measured in square units. (Think of taking a box apart at its seams. You get a flat, two-dimensional object, right?)

And what about the perimeter of a two-dimensional figure, like the wedge-shaped flowerbed? Is that measured in square units? No again. Because perimeter is length, it's measured in units. (Think of stretching out the curved garden hose. You get a line, right?)

Summer Math

Good news! Rick landed a great summer job doing landscaping for a local company. All day long, he hauls mulch, cuts lawns, and trims shrubbery.

Bad news! When getting out of the truck one morning, Rick slipped on a puddle of water and fell. His left leg is in a cast—and he can't do the landscaping any longer.

Good news! Rick's boss also runs a gardening supply business, and his office assistant is out on maternity leave. Rick can keep working at the company, taking orders for mulch, topsoil, compost, and gravel.

Bad news! Rick isn't sure he can do the math required for the job. He's fine with folks who know exactly how many cubic yards of mulch they need. But he's worried about the customers who don't know how to figure that out for themselves.

On day 1, he gets his first test.

Susan has recently lost her job. She used to have a landscaping service take care of her weekly lawn trimming and biannual mulch delivery. But this year, she needs to cut some costs, and the landscaping service is at the top of the list of luxuries that have to go.

Her hubby will take over the mowing and the task of spreading the mulch, but she'll be responsible for ordering the mulch. She calls Rick, who has to help her figure out how much mulch she'll need.

Rick knows one thing for sure: Even though mulch covers a two-dimensional space, it's measured in cubic yards. That's because, once it's spread, the mulch itself has a thickness. (He reminds himself of this by thinking of the mulch layer as a really, really short rectangular box.) Typically, his boss recommends a layer of 4" of mulch for ordinary flower gardens.

"What are the dimensions of your flower beds?" Rick asks Susan. She tells him that they're 24' by 10' and 28' by 11'. Rick suggests that it would be best for him to do the math and then call Susan back. She agrees.

On a piece of paper, Rick writes down the dimensions of Susan's flower beds.

$$24' \times 10'$$
$$28' \times 11'$$

Because the mulch must be 4" deep, he needs to add another dimension.

$$24' \times 10' \times 4"$$
$$28' \times 11' \times 4"$$

It's a good thing that Rick included the units in his notes. Otherwise, he might have been tempted to think of 4" as 4', and that would have made his answer way, way too large.

Rick needs to have all of his measurements in the same units. But should he use feet or inches? His final answer will have to be in cubic yards, so he decides that using feet is the best option, because it will be easier for him to convert cubic feet into cubic yards than to convert cubic inches into cubic yards.

He knows that 4 inches is the same as 0.33333 . . . feet. He decides that rounding to the nearest hundredth is probably just fine, so he substitutes 0.33 for 0.3333. . . . And he plugs in the new number:

$$24' \times 10' \times 0.33$$
$$28' \times 11' \times 0.33$$

Then he multiplies and gets 79.2 ft³ and 101.64 ft³.

These two numbers are the amounts of mulch needed for the two flower beds, so Rick can add them together to find the total amount of mulch he needs.

$$79.2 \text{ ft}^3 + 101.64 \text{ ft}^3 = 180.84 \text{ ft}^3$$

But he's not finished yet. Rick's boss sells mulch in cubic yards, not in cubic feet. Rick needs to make one last conversion before calling Susan back.

Rick knows that there's a conversion chart somewhere in the office, but darned if he can find it. So he has to think a little bit more.

One cubic foot is like a 1 foot by 1 foot by 1 foot cube. That could also be expressed as $1 \cdot 1 \cdot 1 = 1$. And 1 cubic yard is like a 1 yard by 1 yard by 1 yard cube. How many of the first cubes will fit into the second?

The answer is 27. That's because the cubic yard is 3 feet by 3 feet by 3 feet, or

$$3 \cdot 3 \cdot 3 = 27$$

(Another way to write this is $3^3 = 27$.)

Because there are 27 ft^3 in 1 yd^3, Rick needs to divide his original answer by 27 to find out how many cubic yards Susan will need to order.

$$180.84 \div 27 = 6.69777 \ldots$$

Rounding up, Rick sees that Susan needs 7 yd^3 of mulch, and he feels much better about his math abilities.

Grow, Baby, Grow!

Many gardeners use a little fertilizer to help their baby lettuces and carrots grow. These come in a variety of applications—from granules to sprays to concentrated liquids that must be mixed with water before they are sprayed.

Perfect Petunia liquid plant fertilizer is one of the latter. It must be mixed with water before it can be sprayed on plants. The directions say to mix at a rate of 8 fluid ounces per 16 gallons.

What if your sprayer only holds 1 gallon? How much Perfect Petunia fertilizer should you add to the sprayer?

A ratio comes in handy here. Eight fluid ounces of fertilizer to 16 gallons of water, or 8:16, is how we could express this. If you remember, ratios can also be expressed as fractions: $\frac{8}{16}$ is still another way to say this.

To find the correct ratio of fertilizer to water, you start by recording what you know. You know that the ratio is $\frac{8}{16}$, with 16 being the number of gallons. You know your sprayer holds 1 gallon. So what you have is a ratio with an unknown, like this: x:1. In order to solve the problem, these two ratios must be equal. And, ta-da! That means you create a proportion. (A proportion is nothing more than two ratios set equal to one another.)

$$\frac{8}{16} = \frac{x}{1}$$

To find x, you have to isolate it. And that requires cross multiplication in this case—just multiply the numerator of one fraction by the denominator of the other.

$$8 \cdot 1 = x \cdot 16$$
$$8 = 16x$$

We still haven't isolated x, but we're closer. Next, divide each side of the equation by 16.

$$\frac{8}{16} = \frac{16x}{16}$$
$$\tfrac{1}{2} = x$$

That means you'll use ½ fluid ounce per 1 gallon of water for your sprayer.

Word by Word

Using math in everyday life is nothing like solving those rows of algebra equations you had in high school. Formulas and equations don't magically fall from the sky. And even if you don't need an equation, how do you know when to do even the simple stuff, like add, subtract, multiply, or divide?

Simple. Read the clues.

Each math problem has some clues in it that tell you exactly what to do. You just need to know what they are. Here's a short list of words and phrases that serve as clues to the five most commonly used operations.

Addition: sum, total, in all, perimeter

Subtraction: difference, how much more, exceed

Multiplication: product, total, area, times

Division: share, distribute, quotient, average, half, ratio

Equals: same as, is the same amount, costs

Stocking the Pond

Gary has just bought a great house. It even has a pond in the backyard! There's not much landscaping to be done, but the pond is empty, and Gary would like to put in a few of those big goldfish he's seen at the Japanese restaurant downtown.

Gary doesn't even know that these fish are called koi. But he is smart enough to call One Fish, Two Fish, the local experts in aquariums and garden ponds.

"How big is your pond?" says the guy who answers the phone. Gary has no idea.

"Well, what shape is it? Round? Kidney? Rectangular?"

Aha! A question Gary can answer. "It's round," he beams.

The fishmonger explains that Gary needs to know the surface area of the pond before he can purchase the fish. That's because the surface area determines how many fish can survive in a pond.

Gary hangs up and grabs his tape measure. He's not quite sure how he can find surface area, but he knows that his pond is circular. If he measures from one side to the other, he's sure to get something he can use.

The width of the pond is 10 feet. But from that measurement, how can Gary find the surface area?

Even though the pond itself is three-dimensional, the surface area of the water is the area of the circle itself. And the area of a circle is found with this formula:

$$A = \pi r^2$$

With dim memories of "pi are square" ringing in his mind, Gary recalls that π can be estimated by using 3.14. He also recalls that r is the radius of the circle. But he doesn't know what the radius is.

Then Gary has another *aha!* moment. He measures the *diameter* of the pond, which is twice the radius. If the diameter is 10 feet, then the radius of the pond is 5 feet. Now he can use the formula.

$$A = \pi \cdot 5^2$$

Should Gary multiply π and 5 first or square 5 first? Another *aha!* moment. Gary remembers the order of operations—exponents are calculated before multiplication is performed.

$$A = \pi \cdot 25 \text{ ft}$$
$$A = 3.14 \cdot 25 \text{ ft}$$
$$A = 78.5 \text{ ft}^2$$

Gary knows now that the surface area of the water in his pond is 78.5 ft^2. He calls One Fish, Two Fish back. The guy on the phone tells him a little more about the fish he's interested in.

1. If he needs to round the surface area, he should round down. (It's better to have too few fish than too many.) So that 78.5-ft^2 measurement should be rounded down to 78 ft^2, not up to 79 ft^2.
2. Gary should purchase half an inch (or ½ inch) of koi per square foot of surface area.
3. The shop has 12-inch koi for sale.

Between Gary and the fish guy, the math is a breeze:

$$\tfrac{1}{2} \cdot 78 = 39 \text{ inches of fish}$$
$$39 \div 12 = 3.25, \text{ or (again rounding down) 3 fish}$$

By the end of the spring, Gary's pond is swimming with gorgeous koi, which love eating mosquitoes and somehow escape the clutches of the neighbor's cat.

Rounding Rules

There's no need to feel penned in by the elementary rounding rules you memorized all those years ago—such as "round up if the next digit is 5 or greater" or "round down if the next digit is less than 5." Sometimes rounding up makes more sense than rounding down, and vice versa—no matter what your math book said.

Take Gary's fish, for example. Normally, he would round 78.5 up to 79. But as his fish expert recommended, it's better to have more space for the fish than to crowd too many fish into too small a habitat.

Then again, if your teenage son decides to put away 50% of his lawn-mowing earnings, he'll save a lot faster if he rounds all of his deposits up to the nearest dollar, rather than down.

Just one more example of the flexibility of math.

7

In the Craft Room: Measure Twice, Cut Once

Some folks are the crafty type. They play with paper, fabric, beads, wood. They can recreate the Mona Lisa in glitter or make their own ceramic dishes. On birthdays and holidays, they give handmade soaps (created from herbs they've grown in their own garden, naturally), knitted tea cozies, and birdfeeders that resemble Westminster Abbey.

At a craft fair, they're the ones examining the wares carefully—not to buy, mind you. No, they're mentally taking them apart, in order to re-create them at home, perhaps out of completely different materials.

They have an attic full of fringe, fabric, and foam, just waiting for the right project. And they know all the differences between white glue, wood glue, and rubber cement.

You hate them.

But even though there's much to envy, there's no need for hard feelings. There's room in the world for all sorts of crafters. Maybe you're only interested in putting your grandmother's sewing machine to work hemming up all those pants your taller sister gave you. Or you may want to learn how to make new candles from the stubs you have stuck in your utility drawer.

Whatever your goals, math sneaks into most projects in the craft room. So grab your glue gun and a sharp pair of scissors. Let's get crafty.

A Good Yarn

Knitting and crocheting have hit the big time. With weekly knitting circles and yarn shops cropping up like mushrooms after a long rain, you can't even go to church without hearing the clicking of needles. Who knew that granny squares could be hip again?

The geometry of yarn work is pretty simple, especially if you're making a scarf or a blanket. (Rectangles are simple.) Every good knitter and crocheter has a few easy math skills at the tips of her needles and hooks.

Last week, Ann found the most gorgeous yarn on sale at her favorite yarn shop, Knits for Ewe. And she has just the project for it—a simple crocheted scarf.

The problem is that the sale wasn't really that wonderful. She could afford only 4 skeins of it, and her pattern calls for 6 skeins.

No matter. She can make the scarf smaller for her goddaughter, Jasmine, who just turned 5. It'll make a great gift when she visits Jasmine and her family in November. Ann decides to leave the width of the scarf the same and reduce the length.

But how can she change the pattern? Her best bet is to do a little math.

Proportions are just the thing in this situation. They are ideal for showing the relationships among four numbers. (A ratio is a way to compare two numbers; proportions are just ratios on steroids.)

Her pattern tells Ann the relationship between the number of skeins and the length of the finished scarf. (She's already checked her gauge, so she knows she can trust the size.) The pattern calls for 6 skeins of yarn, and the finished scarf will be 66 inches long.

Ann writes that information as a ratio:

$$\frac{6}{66}$$

She has 4 skeins of yarn, but she doesn't know how long her scarf should be. Therefore, she creates another ratio to represent this information, using s as her stand-in for the length of the shortened scarf:

$$\frac{4}{s}$$

Now she's ready to create the proportion, and it is

$$\frac{6}{66} = \frac{4}{s}$$

Ann looks carefully at the equation she's created. Does it really express an equality? She needs the numerators to be "like items" (the numbers of skeins) and the denominators to be "like items" (the lengths of the scarves). Satisfied, she moves on.

To solve the proportion, Ann just needs to cross multiply. She'll have to multiply the numerator of the first ratio by the denominator of the second ratio and the numerator of the second ratio by the denominator of the first ratio. (That's a lot easier *done* than *said*, actually!)

$$\frac{6}{66} = \frac{4}{s}$$
$$6s = 4 \cdot 66$$
$$6s = 264$$

Now she can solve for x by dividing each side of the equation by 6.

$$\frac{6s}{6} = \frac{264}{6}$$
$$s = 44 \text{ inches}$$

Aha! Her finished scarf will be 44 inches long.

Now that the math is out of the way, Ann can get to work.

Sample Size

Open up any how-to-make-cute-yarn-thingies book, and you'll first be instructed to make a gauge or tension swatch.

Here's the thing: Some of us are tightly wound; others of us are *laissez-faire* personified. And those personality traits show up in our yarn work. If you crochet too tightly, a scarf you make might not be long enough to wrap around your boyfriend's chilly neck. And if you knit too loosely, a medium-sized sweater might fit a linebacker.

But yarn people are an accepting bunch. There's no need for self-help books or therapy. Be yourself! And also know yourself.

Before starting a project, knit or crochet a sample, using the same yarn and the same needle or hook size. The pattern will tell you how long a certain number of stitches should be. For example, a 10-cm knitted square might need to be 22 stitches and 30 rows, using 4-mm needles.

When you're finished, compare your sample with the gauge on the pattern. Too small? Up your needle or hook size. Too big? Go down a size or two.

Math? Sew What!

It's all Heidi Klum's fault.

Reggie had never been interested in sewing, much less fashion, until Klum brought burgeoning fashion designers to the small screen. He eagerly awaited new seasons—and new episodes—of the fashion design contest. And soon, he was dragging his mother's Singer sewing machine up from the basement.

He carefully oiled its parts and collected tools from local yard sales—a good pair of shears, a quilter's rule, a tape measure, and even a jar full of old buttons.

But what is Reggie—a newcomer to the art of fabric—going to sew first? His glance lands on the ratty sofa pillows he's had for years. Sure, they were pretty when he first bought them, but now, not so much. Plus they're square, which makes for easy lines and measurements.

Pillow covers it is.

Doing the Calculations

First, he needs to know how much fabric he'll need. Reggie hunts for his new tape measure. The pillows are indeed square, measuring 1½' by 1½'. He pulls out a piece of paper and sketches a simple square. Then he labels his drawing.

Easy enough. For each pillow, he needs two pieces of fabric measuring 1½' by 1½'—one piece for the back and one piece for the front. Because he is making two pillows, he'll need four pieces all together.

But then Reggie remembers seam allowances. If he's going to sew the fabric together, he needs to make room for the seams. But how much room? On a website for beginning sewers, he learns that seam allowances are typically ⅝". He looks again at his sketch, thinking about where the seams will go.

Reggie knows there are four seams in each of his pillows—one for each side—so he needs to add ⅝" to each side of the square. Doing some calculations, this is what he comes up with:

Front and back pieces of each pillow = ⅝" + 1½' + ⅝"

Ugh. Reggie notices two things right away: Not only is he dealing with mixed numbers *and* fractions, but he's also got two different units of measurement: inches and feet. He's going to have to do some conversions. He decides on inches.

$$1½' = 1' + ½'$$
$$1' = 12"$$
$$½' = 12" \cdot ½, \text{ or } 6"$$
$$1½' = 12" + 6"$$
$$1½' = 18"$$

(Wait! You say there's an easier way to do this? Yes, you can simply multiply 1.5 by 12. You'll get the same answer. But know this: Fractions are huge in sewing. Getting some practice with them is not a bad idea if you have sewing aspirations yourself.)

Reggie revisits his addition problem, this time using 18" in place of 1½'. And now that everything is in the same unit of measurement, he doesn't need to include those annoying little unit marks.

$$⅝ + 18 + ⅝$$

Clearly, Reggie still has work to do. He can get a common denominator for all of the fractions. Or he can try a different process, to make things easier on himself.

Reggie had the problem arranged this way because he was picturing his pillow: seam allowance + size of pillow + seam allowance. But this is addition, so he doesn't *have* to add in that order. It makes more sense for him to add the fractions together first and then see what he can do.

$$\tfrac{5}{8} + \tfrac{5}{8} + 18$$

$$\frac{10}{8} + 18$$

Now he's faced with another choice. $\frac{10}{8}$ is an improper fraction—in other words, it's larger than 1. Should he change it to a mixed number—a whole number and a fraction? He decides to do so. That's because it's pretty straightforward to add a mixed number to a whole number.

To change an improper fraction to a mixed number, just divide the numerator by the denominator. The answer is your whole number, and the remainder is the numerator of the fraction part. The denominator stays the same.

He scribbles these steps in the margin.

$$\frac{10}{8} = 1\frac{2}{8}$$

But wait. There's something up with Reggie's answer. The fraction of the mixed number isn't in its simplest form. That's not necessarily a huge deal, but this fraction is easy to reduce. All he needs to do is find a common factor for both the numerator and the denominator and then divide each by that number. The 1 just comes along for the ride.

$$1\frac{2}{8} = 1\frac{2 \div 2}{8 \div 2} = 1\frac{1}{4}$$

Thus Reggie's seam allowances add up to 1¼". He can finish the problem now:

$$1¼ \text{ inches} + 18 \text{ inches} = 19¼ \text{ inches}$$

That means Reggie needs four squares of fabric that measure 19¼ inches on all four sides.

Putting the Calculations to Use

Buying the fabric is the next step. At Yard by Yard, Reggie heads to the decorator fabrics, looking for something sturdy, without a lot of stretch.

Two fabrics catch his eye: a lime-green polka dot on cream, and a fuchsia paisley. The polka-dot fabric is 54" wide, and the paisley is 48" wide. This is where his calculator will come in handy.

How many pillows can Reggie fit along the width of the fabric?

Each pillow is 19¼" wide. He knows he needs to divide the width of the fabric by that number. Instead of trying to convert the ¼" to a decimal, Reggie just rounds down to 19. Dealing with the 54"-wide fabric first, he divides:

$$54" \div 19" = 2.8$$

Now the 48"-wide fabric:

$$48" \div 19" = 2.5$$

Reggie can get only two pieces across each of the fabrics. Which one should he buy? He'll have less fabric left over with the second one, and besides, he always thought that room could use a punch of pink. Fuchsia it is!

But how many yards? The length of the side of his sketch will help here, too. He needs pieces for two pillows. Because two pieces will fit on the 19" length of 48"-wide fabric, he needs just two 19" lengths (19" • 2 = 38").

But fabric is sold by the yard, so he still needs to convert again. How many yards is 38"?

There are 36 inches in 1 yard (12 inches in a foot and 3 feet in a yard: 3 • 12 = 36). Reggie needs to divide the number of inches he needs by 36 to find out how many yards he needs.

39 inches ÷ 36 inches = 1.09 yards or 1 yard 3 inches

Convert the Converted

Whether you're scrapbooking, welding, sewing, or woodworking, you may find yourself dealing with metric units occasionally. This handy chart will help you convert metric units to standard units.

1 in.	25.4 mm	2.5 cm
1 ft	0.305 m	30.5 cm
1 yd	0.914 m	91.4 cm

Knowing some basic fraction-to-decimal conversions is really helpful, too.

$7/8$	0.875
$4/5$	0.8
$3/4$	0.75
$5/8$	0.625
$3/5$	0.6
$1/2$	0.5
$2/5$	0.4
$3/8$	0.375
$1/4$	0.25
$1/5$	0.2
$1/8$	0.125

He needs a little more than 1 yard, but not much. Reggie decides on 1¼ yards.

Now all he needs is a spool of thread, some needles, and a few hours of free time.

Heidi Klum, here he comes!

Side to Side

Fabrics have standard widths that vary by type of fabric. Here's a typical list of fabric widths, although they may vary from manufacturer to manufacturer.

Type of Fabric	Possible Widths
Decorator fabric	48" and 54"
Fashion fabric	36", 45", and 60"
Quilting fabric	42" to 44"

If you're lucky enough to score vintage fabrics, you might find some even stranger widths.

By the way, because width is measured in inches, use inches when you convert your measurements. It's much easier to figure out what you need if you're already working with like units.

Cherish the Love

Mary has decided to take up scrapbooking. She's a terrific photographer, and she'd like to highlight her art in some special ways. Besides, her mother's birthday is coming up, and she'd cry if she received a scrapbook of photos of Mary's kids.

Any new hobby requires materials, and scrapbooking is no exception. Mary picks up an album, some acid-free paper, adhesives, and a few nice pens. Then she starts thinking about the types of pages she wants to build.

Mary loves spreadsheets, so she opens one up and starts typing. She read somewhere that a two-page spread shouldn't have more than 10 photos. She can break this rule if she wants, but it sounds like a good frame of reference.

Mary starts categorizing her photos, and here's what she ends up with:

CATEGORIES	NUMBER OF PHOTOS	NUMBER OF PAGES
The Kids: Ella	20	
The Kids: Mabel	15	
The Kids: Josh	18	
Halloween	10	
Beach vacations	48	
Holidays with the folks	32	
Road trip out west	12	

Clearly, she's going to need more pages for some subjects than for others.

There's something else Mary needs to consider. Her final single-page count must be divisible by 4. That's so she doesn't have any blank pages.

Using trial and error, Mary finagles the number of photos and the number of pages until she comes up with this count.

CATEGORIES	NUMBER OF PHOTOS	NUMBER OF PAGES
The kids: Ella	20	4
The kids: Mabel	15	4
The kids: Josh	18	4
Halloween	10	2
Beach vacations	48	6
Holidays with the folks	32	6
Road trip out west	12	4

Using her spreadsheet application to total the pages, she finds that she's planned for 30 pages. But that's a problem. Thirty is not a multiple of 4. In other words, 4 doesn't divide evenly into 30.

Mary thinks a moment. What multiple of 4 is closest to 30? Well, 28 and 32 are both close to 30. Should she add 2 pages or subtract 2 pages?

Mary thinks again. Then she picks up her copy of *Moby Dick* from the coffee table. There's the cover—just like the cover of her album—and the title page, then hundreds of 2-page spreads, and finally the back page.

Mary hadn't considered the first and last pages!

It makes sense for her to add 2 pages. That way, she can do a nice title page and wrap things up at the end—maybe with a cute picture of grandma and the kids.

She has a plan. Now all Mary needs to do is figure out the differences between glues, adhesive tapes, and photo corners.

Opposites Attract

A *multiple* is what you get when you multiply two numbers. (What you get is also called a product.)

Any multiple of a number is evenly divisible by that number—which means there won't be anything left over. So, if you multiply 9 (let's say) by 3 to get a multiple of 27, you'll find that the multiple (27) is divisible by that number (9). And there are no pesky fractions left over. That makes sense, because you used 9 to get the product in the first place. Obviously, you can use 9 to divide the product.

Multiplication and division are opposite, but they're related operations. Let's look at another example:

$$4 \cdot 6 = 24$$

So, 24 is a multiple of 4 and 6, because we multiplied 4 and 6 to get that product.

And according to our rule, that means the multiple (24) is evenly divisible by 4 (the quotient, or answer, is 6) and also is evenly divisible by 6 (in which case the quotient is 4).

But wait! There's more! A *factor* is a number that divides evenly into another number.

$$4 \cdot 6 = 24$$

So 4 and 6 are factors of 24.

Can you think of another factor of 24?

And if you multiply two (or more) factors, you get a multiple. Which is how we started this whole discussion.

Get the Picture

If your photos are stored electronically, you can size them easily using software. But before that software existed, book publishers, newspaper designers, and even yearbook editors had to depend on good old proportions to blow up or shrink photos. And in fact, this is exactly how image software works today.

Remember, a proportion is a pair of equal ratios. If you change one of the numerators, you have to change its corresponding denominator in the same way. Otherwise, the ratios will no longer be equal.

Let's say you have a photograph that is 6 inches tall by 4 inches wide. You'd like to enlarge it so that the width is 6 inches. If you change the width without changing the height, you'll have an odd-looking photo. So if you change the height proportionally to the change in the width, what will the height of the new photograph be?

First set up the proportion, using the heights as the numerators and the widths as the denominators.

$$\frac{6}{4} = \frac{x}{6}$$

Then cross-multiply and solve for x.

$$36 = 4x$$
$$9 = x$$

The picture must be 9 inches tall.

What if you set up the proportion with the widths as the numerators and the heights as the denominators?

$$\frac{4}{6} = \frac{6}{x}$$
$$4x = 36$$
$$x = 9$$

How about that—the same answer. Math *is* flexible!

Economies of Crafting

Before pulling out the sewing machine or setting up the table saw, ask yourself, "Does it make more sense to buy what I'm about to make?"

You may want the experience of building something from scratch. But you also may need to keep a little change in your pocket. It's always a good idea to consider what your craft will cost the family budget.

Rita loves Halloween, and she loves making her kids' costumes. This year, her 10-year-old daughter has requested a velvet-like cape and gown so that she can dress as some obscure character from her favorite novel about magical kids.

The pattern Rita is using calls for 7 yards of fabric, 2 fancy fasteners, and 3 yards of fringe. Looking at the Sunday circular for the local fabric store, she sees that crushed panne velvet is on sale for $2.99 per yard and the fringe is priced at $4 per yard. Rita guesses that the fasteners are about $5 each. To estimate her costs, she adds everything together:

$$(7 \cdot \$2.99) + (3 \cdot \$4) + (2 \cdot \$5)$$

(In case you lost track, that's 7 yards of fabric at $2.99 per yard, 3 yards of fringe at $4 per yard, and 2 frog clasps at $5 each.)

$$\$20.93 + \$12 + \$10 = \$42.93$$

A terrifying price!

Rita is starting to think that a trip to a thrift shop might be a better investment of her time and money. Sometimes doing it yourself just isn't worth it.

OMG! TMI!

On math worksheets from school, you have exactly the information you need. In real life, though, you have to decide which numbers are relevant—and how. That's not always as simple as it sounds.

Tad wants to build a birdhouse out of scrap wood. He's interested in attracting chickadees, so he does some research, and this is what he learns:

Base of the interior: 4" by 4"
Height of the interior: 10"
Distance of entrance from the floor: 8"
Diameter of entrance: 1⅛"
Height above ground: 6' to 15'

Which of the pieces of information on this list will he use to build the birdhouse?

Basically, Tad will be constructing a box with a big hole drilled into it. To figure out how much wood he'll need, he uses the dimensions of the box: 4" by 4" by 10". Those dimensions tell him the dimensions of each side.

each of 4 sides: 4" by 10"
top and base: 4" by 4"

Tad will need to cut four pieces of wood that measure 4" by 10" and two pieces that measure 4" by 4". (Any box has six sides.)

The next two measurements in his list tell Tad where and how large to drill the entrance to the birdhouse.

But that last bit of information? It's not relevant. It is only *after* he's built the birdhouse that Tad needs to know how high to install it.

At the Bank: Income Minus Expenses Equals Happiness (or Misery)

Old-timers remember the good old days when they paid their bills with a check and trusted the local bank to give good interest rates and honest loans. They had a pension and Social Security, so they didn't play the stock market or invest in a 401(k) plan.

Those times are long gone.

These days, virtually everyone invests in Wall Street. Pensions—and maybe even Social Security—will soon appear only in history books. Credit and debit cards have replaced cash. And checkbooks? What are those?

Managing finances is probably the most math-intensive part of modern daily life. And a lot hangs on those calculations: your retirement, your kids' college tuition, your salary.

Unlike gardening or finding the sale price on a big-screen TV, this stuff can make you or break you. It literally pays to have a good handle on financial math.

Budget Basics

Dad harped about a lot of things. Have you studied for your test? Did you take out the trash? Are you changing the oil in your car? Did you call your mother? Have you drawn up a budget?

But that last question is one of those times when he was absolutely right. You oughta have a budget. Yep, they're a pain you know where, but budgets can keep you on track financially.

It's New Year's Day, and Darrel is pondering his resolutions over a bowl of black-eyed peas. For sure, he wants to reach level 65 in *Purple Heart: World at War*. And he wants to ask out that cute girl in the apartment next door.

But Darrel is also sick and tired of worrying about money. He's got a good job as a computer programmer, but for some reason, he's still ending up with too many bills at the end of the month. Last year, he had to sell his first-edition *Spiderman* comic to pick up a little extra cash. He knows he needs to add a really, really boring New Year's resolution to his list: keeping a personal finances budget.

He vaguely remembers what his high school consumer math teacher told him about budgets. At least he remembers that there are three parts: income, regular expenses, and occasional expenses. His income should be greater than all of his expenses put together.

He writes the name of the month at the top of the page, March, and then adds his current monthly income: $2,655.

He's careful to put in his take-home income, not his before-tax income, because that's all he can spend.

Now he brainstorms all of his regular expenses, including his weekly comic store purchases. Some of his expenses, such as his electric bill, vary a bit from month to month, but he adds up the last year's worth and divides by 12 to get a monthly average.

EXPENSES

ITEM	COST	ITEM	COST
Rent	$800	College loans	$200
Electricity	$145	Gas	$100
Water	$21	Comics	$100
Cell	$80	Groceries	$400
Internet	$42	Entertainment	$200
Satellite	$100	Clothing	$100
Car payment	$360		
Total			$2,648

So far, so good. It looks like Darrel is living within his means, but what will happen when he adds in his occasional expenses? He brainstorms again, consulting his online banking records for guidance.

OCCASIONAL EXPENSES

ITEM	COST	TOTAL PER YEAR
Car insurance	$450 every quarter	$1800
Comic book conventions	$4,200 per year	$4,200
Professional association dues	$500 per year	$500
Dojo fees	$275 per semester	$550
Gifts	$170 per year	$170
Total		$7,220

He divides that total by 12 to get his average monthly expense: $601.67.

In the Red

When you spend more than you make, the totals in your budget will be negative. And that's for a simple math reason: When you subtract a larger number from a smaller number, the answer is negative.

Let's say you brought home $3,114 last month, but you spent $3,788. To find the difference, you need to subtract. But the answer will be negative.

$$\$3,114 - \$3,788$$
$$-\$674$$

An ordinary calculator will handle this problem easily, but if you're using pen and paper, you'll need to set up the problem a little differently. Put the larger number on top and the smaller number on the bottom. And then subtract. The key is to remember that the answer will be negative.

Some Budget Averages

If you're wondering whether you're spending too much of your income on certain line items in your budget, check out this advice from budgeting gurus.

- Groceries should account for about 18% of your monthly gross income.
- Housing should cost no more than 28% to 33% of your monthly gross income.
- You should be saving at least 10% to 20% of your monthly gross income.

Speaking of savings, you should have at least 4 months of your monthly take-home income in the bank—in an account that you can get to easily. This amount serves as an emergency fund, for when the pipes burst or, worse, you find yourself on the unemployment line.

He adds his regular and occasional expenses together: $2,648 + 601.67 = $3,249.67. That's more than his monthly take-home pay! He's going to have cut back. It takes Darrel only a few moments to recalibrate his budget. He's going to reduce the number of comic book conventions he goes to, and he's going to cut down his satellite television expenses. He notices that he can put some money each month into his languishing savings account. And if, at the end of the year, he gets that raise he's been expecting, he can put even more away for a rainy day.

This little bit of math gives Darrel a boost of confidence—enough confidence that he picks up the phone and calls his cute neighbor.

The Great Negotiator

One way to balance out your budget is to increase your income. But is a higher salary always the best—or most reasonable—option? Negotiating your salary package, which includes vacation time, benefits, and perhaps even commissions, is all part of the equation.

Congratulations! You just landed a brand-new job as human resources director for Darling Day Care Centers.

But before you settle into the work of managing teachers, assistants, and lunch preparation staff for this 40-center company, you need to negotiate your pay. (And you thought the job interview was tough!)

They've offered you a $48,000 salary, which is not bad. Still, you're hoping they can go up to $50,000.

If they can't, you have an idea. An extra two weeks of vacation could be a pretty good deal. But how does giving you two more weeks of vacation compare to upping their offer by $2,000?

To find out, you need to know the monetary value of two extra vacation weeks. And that number depends on your hourly rate.

Being on salary means you'll be paid for holidays or any vacation taken. So even though you won't be working 40 hours a week, 52 weeks a year, you're paid for that time. For the entire year, you'll be compensated for working

$$40 \cdot 52 = 2,080 \text{ hours}$$

Now you can find your hourly wage with simple division:

$$\$48,000 \div 2,080 = \$23.08$$

So how much would the company be paying you to lounge on a tropical beach? Multiply your hourly rate by the number of working hours in two weeks (or 80 hours).

$$\$23.08 \cdot 80 = \$1,846.40$$

Huh. The cost of an extra two weeks of vacation is pretty darned close to the extra $2,000 you'd like to see in your salary. You can live with that.

It's time to negotiate.

Wicked Debt

Glenda may be the Good Witch, but she's not so good with her money. She really, really, really wanted that Bubble Transportation Vehicle (BTV). What better way to impress the Munchkins *and* make it from her apartment to Munchkinland in 30 seconds flat?

But the darned thing cost a lot of money. Money that she didn't have. Always the optimist, she simply pulled out her Bank of Oz gold card and said, "Swipe it!"

Now good Glenda is in trouble. The interest rate on her card is 18%, and she's worried that she'll never pay off the debt.

Glenda has decided to get tough on herself. She really needs to pay off her credit card in 3 years, and she has $17,000 to go. What monthly payment should she make?

She may drive a BTV, but Glenda doesn't have bubbles on the brain. She uses the monthly payment formula (from Chapter 2) to find her answer.

$$M = P\left(\frac{r}{1-(1\div r)^{-n}}\right)$$

(Did you notice that the formula is slightly different here than in Chapter 2? That's because of the way the variables are defined. Keep reading, and you'll see that r is the *monthly* interest rate in this version of the formula.)

First, she needs to understand the variables. Glenda has used this formula before—to find the monthly payments on that brand new BMW that she thought was a good idea a few years ago. (Dumb thing didn't go very fast!) Anyway, she knows that

M is the monthly payment
P is the amount owed on the loan
r is the monthly interest rate
n is the number of months in the period of the loan

With her favorite pink, feathered pen, she gets to work, defining her variables:

$M = ?$
$P = \$17{,}000$
$r = 18\% \div 12 = 0.015$
$n = 3 \cdot 12 = 36$

Now she can use the formula.

$$M = P\left(\frac{r}{1-(1+r)^{-n}}\right)$$

$$M = 17{,}000\left(\frac{0.015}{1-(1+0.015)^{-36}}\right)$$

Glenda has a good handle on her order of operations, thanks to **P**lease **E**xcuse **M**y **D**ear **A**unt **S**ally. And she remembers that $x^{-n} = \dfrac{1}{x^n}$. So even without a scientific calculator—it didn't come in purple—she can find the solution.

$$M = 17{,}000\left(\frac{0.015}{1-\left(1.015\right)^{-36}}\right)$$

First, she deals with that negative exponent.

$$M = 17{,}000\left(\frac{0.015}{1-\left(\dfrac{1}{1.015^{36}}\right)}\right)$$

Now Glenda finds 1.015^{36}.

$$M = 17{,}000\left(\frac{0.015}{1-\left(\dfrac{1}{1.709}\right)}\right)$$

Next, she starts handling the parentheses, beginning with the one in the denominator of the fraction.

$$M = 17{,}000\left(\frac{0.015}{1-0.585}\right)$$

She finishes off the calculations in the denominator:

$$M = 17{,}000\left(\frac{0.015}{0.415}\right)$$

And divides.

$$M = 17{,}000 \cdot 0.036$$

Finally, she can multiply to find her monthly payment.

$$M = \$612$$

"Well!" Glenda breathily exclaims. "That seems manageable!" She makes plans to skip her weekly tea with the mayor of Munchkinland and reduce her hoopskirt budget by half.

"That should do it!" she twinkles. And hops in her BTV to share the good news with the Wizard.

Interesting Formula

If interest were not compounded, these formulas would be a heck of a lot simpler. When you compound interest, you earn interest on the interest.

Compound interest is great for savings accounts, but not so wonderful for credit card balances. When interest is compounded on debt, you are *paying* interest on the interest. But when the interest on your savings is compounded, you *earn* interest on the interest.

Simple interest is the opposite: not so great for savings, but terrific for credit card balances. You *earn* less on a savings account earning simple interest than on an account earning compound interest. But you *pay* less on a debt that is earning simple interest than on one earning compound interest.

To find the amount due on a loan that earns compound interest, you need to know a few things: the amount of the loan, the interest rate, and the number of compounding periods. Then you can use this handy-dandy amount-due formula:

$$A = P(1 + r)^n$$

A is the total amount due

P is the principal

r is the interest rate per compounding period

n is the number of compounding periods

That's a lot to think about, but if you break things down, it's not so bad.

You borrowed $3,500 at 6% interest compounded monthly. If you paid off the loan in 1 year, how much did you pay in all?

The principal is $3,500—that's easy enough. But finding the rest of the variables requires a little more work. Because you paid off the loan in a year and the interest is compounded monthly, the number of compounding periods is 12. That means the interest rate per compounding period is 6% ÷ 12, or 0.5%.

$$A = 3,500(1 + 0.005)^{12}$$
$$A = 3,500(1.005)^{12}$$
$$A = 3,500 \cdot 1.06$$
$$A = \$3,710$$

What if you had a simple-interest loan? You'd use this formula instead:

$$I = Prt$$

I is the total amount of interest
P is the principal
r is the interest rate
t is the length of the loan in years

Substituting, you would find

$$I = 3,500 \cdot 0.06 \cdot 1$$
$$I = \$210$$

So you would owe $210 in interest, bringing your total payment to $3,500 + $210, or $3,710.

But about the only place you can get a simple-interest loan is from Mom and Dad.

How Much Debt Is Too Much Debt?

For some folks, any debt is too much. And others swear that the tax break makes having a mortgage worth it. Still others haven't seen the light and are running up their credit card balances as if someone else is going to pick up the tab.

But no matter what your personal philosophy, there is such a thing as too much debt. And it's not just older relatives and nosey neighbors who care. So does your mortgage lender and anyone else who is considering offering you a big loan.

These creditors consider something called your debt-to-income ratio, a simple number that compares the amount of debt you have with the amount of income you bring in.

And it really is simple:

$$\frac{debt}{income}$$

Julian would like to sell his house and move into a smaller place, but he read somewhere that lenders pay attention to a borrower's debt-to-income ratio. He decides to see whether he has anything to worry about.

First, Julian calculates his monthly debt. His obligations include a mortgage payment ($1,068), a car payment ($347), monthly college loan payments ($289), and monthly child support ($1,146).

$$\$1,068 + \$347 + \$289 + \$1,146 = \$2,850$$

Now he needs to find his total monthly income. At his job he grosses $5,900 each month, and he also gets a monthly $250 check from stock dividends. Then there's his yearly $12,000 bonus. He divides this by 12 to spread it out monthly: $12,000 \div 12 = \$1,000$.

$$\$5,900 + \$250 + \$1,000 = \$7,150$$

What is Julian's debt-to-income ratio?

$$\frac{debt}{income}$$

$$\frac{2,850}{7,150} = 0.40 = 40\%$$

For obvious reasons, Julian wants his debt-to-income ratio to be as small as possible. How small? Lenders like to see it below 36%.

Julian decides he should put house hunting on hold. Mortgage lenders might be more interested once he pays off his car.

Just the Minimum

Most credit cards require a minimum monthly payment that must be paid every month. But here's the thing: These payments are designed to benefit the credit card company, not the cardholder.

The minimum payment is calculated a number of different ways: from 1% of the interest for that period to 4–5% of the total balance. If you pay only the minimum amount each month, you'll be playing right into the credit card company's hands—and shelling out way more interest than otherwise. Here's how it works.

Big Sam hates debt. That's why he's royally peeved at his daughter, Lucy Belle, who came home from college with $6,000 charged on a credit card.

Lucy Belle assures her daddy that as long as she makes the minimum payments, she will be back in the black in no time. Big Sam shakes his head knowingly. And after making Lucy Belle shred the card in his home office, he sits her down for a quick lesson in minimum payments.

Lucy Belle's credit card has 16% interest, and the minimum monthly payment is 2.5% of the balance. Big Sam shows her how to figure out her first minimum monthly payment:

$$\$6,000 \cdot 0.025 = \$150$$

"Well, that's no big deal, Daddy," Lucy Belle says, batting her eyelashes. "If I make the minimum payment every month, I'll be done in 40 months!"

Big Sam realizes that she merely divided $6,000 by $150.

"That's not gonna do it, sugar," he says, shaking his head. Lucy Belle forgot about the interest. Her $150 payment includes some of the balance and a lot of interest. And every month, her minimum payment will go down—just so the credit card company can earn more money.

Because the interest rate is 16%, Lucy Belle will pay 1.333% interest each month. So in the first month, the amount she's paying for interest is

$$\$6,000 \cdot 0.01333 = \$79.98$$

To find out how much of the $150 minimum is going to the balance, she subtracts

$$\$150 - \$79.98 = \$70.02$$

Lucy Belle's new balance is $6,000 - $70.02, or $5,929.98. And she can find the next month's minimum payment from that.

$$\$5,929.98 \cdot 0.025 = \$148.25$$

Lucy Belle quickly figures out her new balance in the second month.

$$\$5,929.98 \cdot 0.01333 = \$79.05$$
$$\$148.25 - \$79.05 = \$69.20$$
$$\$5,929.98 - \$69.20 = \$5,860.78$$

"Oh," she says with a little pout. "I guess I need to do somethin' different, huh?"

"Lemme show you an easier way to figure this out," Big Sam says.

He turns on his computer and pulls up an online credit card calculator. After plugging in the information, he clicks "Calculate," and Lucy Belle gasps. If she makes only those enticingly low minimum payments, it'll take her 254 months to pay off her balance.

"What if I make $150 payments every month?" Lucy Belle asks. "Not just the first month?"

Big Sam enters a fixed monthly payment of $150 into the online calculator. At that rate, it'll take Lucy Belle 58 months to pay off the balance. Much better!

Paying Down Debt

Just listen to the Federal Reserve chiefs address Congress. (You know, Alan Greenspan and Ben Bernanke, the guys the president puts in charge of the economy?) Economists and bean counters love using fancy words for ordinary ideas. Your personal finances are no exception.

Take credit cards as an example.

When you pay down a loan—whether it's a credit card payment, a car payment, or a mortgage payment—you're doing something called *amortization*. Simply put, you're reducing the amount of the loan by making regular payments.

When there's no interest, this is a very simple process. Just subtract the payment to find the new balance. And to figure out the number of payments you'll make, just divide the balance by the payment.

Things get weird, though, when you have to pay interest. And that's one of the reasons for all of the fine print on the back of your credit card statement.

Unless you're paying your balance off each month, each time you make a payment on your credit card debt you're paying principal and interest. And whether you're making fixed or variable payments, these can be shown in an amortization schedule. This is a chart that outlines the amount of interest and principal you're paying each month—and the new balance.

This is exactly what your bank would provide for you—if you were put into a time machine and sent back to the 1950s.

These days, using online calculators, you can customize an amortization schedule with your personal details. If you want to experiment with paying off your debt—by trying various monthly payment amounts—just search for an online credit card calculator. (Try search terms like "credit card calculator.") These tools enable you to plug in different amounts and not get overwhelmed by the math.

Hurray for technology!

Safety Net

Ever wonder how people know they're millionaires? Do they have a million bucks in the bank? Do they own a million-dollar house? Do their debts play a role at all?

The answer to all of these questions could be a simple *yes*. Or not. The issue is *net worth*—and this takes into account the amount of money in savings, what is invested, property, and, yes, debt. Net worth is calculated this way:

Net worth = assets – liabilities

Daddy Warbucks adds up all of his assets—including his three mansions, his dozens of cars, the money he has in the bank and invested on Wall Street, and even the value of his dad's rare coin collection. The total is a whopping $3.7 million.

But he has liabilities, too. These are debts, including the balance on his mortgages, taxes, staff salaries, and Little Orphan Annie's private school tuition. That total is $2.3 million.

So what is Daddy Warbucks's net worth?

$$\$3.7 \text{ million} - \$2.3 \text{ million} = \$1.4 \text{ million}$$

Indeed, Daddy Warbucks is a millionaire. And that's something to sing about.

But should net worth matter to you? Your year-to-year net worth could be a good indication of whether you're staying ahead or getting behind, financially speaking. So checking this out every January, or even when you do your taxes, is a smart idea.

The Golden Years

You may be putting in 60 hours a week at the office, but retirement is in your future. That can be either a thrilling prospect or a terrifying one.

With pensions practically nonexistent and the stability of Social Security in question, quitting your career to take up golf or sit around the house watching *The Golden Girls* reruns may not be a sure thing. It's important to develop a retirement plan—and actually save for those golden years.

But how do you know how much you'll need to retire comfortably? There is lots of advice out there, but one thing is for sure: Doing nothing is a bad idea.

Becky loves selling houses. She loves hunting down new properties and matching them with the perfect buyers. She loves crunching numbers and arranging flowers for open houses.

But Becky loves her grandchildren even more. She'd rather spend her days on the floor playing Barbie or playing soccer in the backyard.

So retirement has been on her mind a lot lately. Her dream is to give up her real estate license in favor of trips to the zoo with little Natalie, John, and Sarah. She just needs to know how to make that happen—and quick.

Becky has not neglected her retirement savings. She'll draw a Social Security check, but it isn't going to cover all of her monthly costs. That's why she's been diligently socking away a percentage of her commissions over the years. Her investment portfolio has a value of $186,000.

But is that enough to retire on? And if not, how much will she need to save before she can say goodbye to real estate?

She signed up for a retirement savings workshop at the local community college. And while there, she learned a few things:

1. She'll need to estimate her retirement expenses and income.
2. The difference of those will be her monthly shortfall.
3. She should have about $15 to $20 in savings to cover each dollar of that shortfall.

The math isn't so bad, she thinks.

The hard part is estimating her retirement expenses. When she retires, she'll lose some expenses, such as the cost of commuting and lunches out. But she'll also add a few items, such as increased health care expenses.

Luckily, Becky has been keeping a budget for years. She knows that her yearly expenses are $55,000. From that, she is able to list her yearly work expenses:

Yearly Work Expenses

Health insurance	$4,500
Wardrobe	$3,000
Commute	$1,000
Lunches	$3,000
Business gifts	$7,000
Social Security and Medicare	$5,000
Retirement savings	$10,000
Professional dues	$250
TOTAL	$33,750

These are expenses she won't have once she retires.

But she will have some new ones, and with a little bit of research, she estimates these costs.

Retirement Expenses	
Medicare premiums	$700
Medical care	$2,000
Long-term care insurance	$1,000
Travel	$3,000
Leisure	$1,000
Clothing	$500
TOTAL	$8,200

How does Becky figure out how much less she'll be spending each year during retirement? First she needs to subtract her retirement expenses from her work expenses.

$$\$33,750 - \$8,200 = \$25,550$$

Then she can subtract this amount from her current yearly expenses to find out how much she'll spend each year during retirement.

$$\$55,000 - \$25,550 = \$29,450$$

So, Becky will need to bring in $29,450 each year to cover her expenses during retirement. She has no pension, but she thinks she can count on Social Security. In fact, her Social Security statement came in the mail last week, showing that her monthly check would be $1,596 if she retired today. Annually, that would be

$$\$1,596 \cdot 12 = \$19,152$$

Clearly, Becky's Social Security check isn't going to cover her yearly expenses. But she does have savings. Is it enough to make up the difference?

Remember, at her financial planning workshop, Becky learned that she should have $15 to $20 in savings for every dollar of her annual shortfall. She can find this shortfall by subtracting her retirement income from her retirement expenses. And then she can multiply.

$$\$29,450 - \$19,152 = \$10,298$$

Becky decides on using the conservative estimate of $20 per dollar. It's much better to estimate high when finances are concerned.

$$\$10,298 \cdot 20 = \$205,960$$

But she only has $186,000 saved. She needs to put away another $19,960 before she can retire in confidence. How long will it take her to save that much?

For this, she needs to go back to her budget. Each year, she saves about $10,000. And she already has $186,000 in investments. Could she save enough in 1 year to retire?

Becky looks through her financial files for her latest investments summary. From that, she learns that she's earning an average of 4% each year on her investments. She uses that figure to estimate what her investments will return next year:

$$\$186,000 \cdot 0.04 = \$7,440$$

With the $10,000 she saves each year, she could have an extra $17,440 at this time next year. That's only $2,520 less than she needs. With a little creative trimming of this year's budget—or by selling an extra house—she could very well be home with her grandbabies by this time next year.

The Rule of 72

Whether you're saving up for a purchase or wondering when you can retire comfortably, it's a good idea to know how quickly your savings will grow. The Rule of 72 tells you how many years it will take to double your money, if the interest it earns is compounded annually.

$$y = 72 \div r$$
$$y \text{ is years}$$
$$r \text{ is the interest rate}$$

You have \$2,500 invested in a money market account earning 1.5% interest each year. How long will it take for your investment to double?

$$y = 72 \div 1.5$$
$$y = 48$$

So if you leave your \$2,500 investment alone, it will become \$5,000 in 48 years. (See why you need to feed your savings?)

You can use the Rule of 72 to shop for savings options. What if you need your \$2,500 to double in 10 years? What interest rate do you need?

$$y = 72 \div r$$

You want your investment to double in 10 years, so substitute 10 for y.

$$10 = 72 \div r$$

Now, it's time for a little algebra. You need to isolate r. To do that, first multiply each side of the equation by r.

$$10r = 72$$

Now you can divide each side of the equation by 10.

$$r = 72 \div 10$$

Finish your division, and you get 7.2. Because of the way this formula is written, your answer is already a percent—so there's no need to move the decimal point.

$$r = 7.2\%$$

But you don't need to go through that entire process each time. It turns out that you can divide 72 by the number of years to find the rate. In other words, $r = 72 \div y$.

But where does this magical formula come from? Why, from the formula for compounding annual interest, of course!

$$A = P(1 + r)^n$$

A is the amount saved

P is principal

r is the annual interest rate

n is the number of years

Remember, you want to solve for *n*, which means isolating it on one side of the equation. And quite frankly, the math involved is messy and complex. But here's a clue. How do you undo exponents?

With logarithms, of course! So if you were deriving (or proving) the Rule of 72, you'd need to use those old friends.

(See why we're skipping it?)

Hitting the Jackpot

Mentally, Lucas is ready to retire. But his bank account says, "No way."

Lucas has a plan. If he plays the same lottery picks every week, he's bound to get lucky, right? The more you play, the better chance you have of winning, right?

Poor Lucas. He's making the same mistake that has troubled players of games of chance and lottery hopefuls for centuries. It's something called the Gambler's Fallacy.

The laws of probability say this: Past events do not change the probability that an event will happen in the future. In other words, Lucas can play those same numbers every week until the day he dies, but each week he has the same chance of winning.

Say it again: exactly the same chance.

Here's an easier way to understand the problems with Lucas's thinking. When you flip a coin, what are your chances that it will come up heads? Yep, 1 to 2, or ½. That's because there are two possible outcomes (heads or tails), and you got one of the outcomes (heads).

Does the chance of getting heads change if you flip the coin over and over again? Actually, no. That's because every single time you flip the coin, your odds of getting heads are still ½.

The same holds true for picking lottery numbers, although the odds of your winning are much, much lower and more complex to figure out:

$$\frac{n!}{(n-r)!\,r!}$$

n is the highest-numbered ball
r is the number of balls chosen

Those variables aren't excited. The exclamation points represent something called a *factorial*. Factorials are not hard to find. But they can produce really, really big numbers.

Here's an easy way to think about factorials. If there are 40 possible lottery-number balls, how many are available after the first pick? 39, right? How many after the second pick? 38. And after the next pick? 37. And so on, and so on. If you keep at this until you get to 1, and then multiply all of the numbers, that's the factorial.

Mathematically speaking—and using a much smaller number—factorials work like this:

$$4! = 4 \cdot 3 \cdot 2 \cdot 1 = 24$$

The lottery that Lucas plays has 40 balls, and he chooses 6 numbers. So, his odds of winning are

$$\frac{40!}{(40-6)! \cdot 6!}$$

$$\frac{2,763,633,600}{720} \text{ (Trust me on this.)}$$

$$3,838,380 \text{ to } 1$$

That's a teeny-tiny chance. And here's the thing. It doesn't matter how often he plays the lottery. His odds are exactly the same from week to week.

Lucas's retirement plan doesn't stand a chance.

A Taxing Proposition

Getting a raise is always a good thing, right? Well, not always. If that extra cash in your paycheck bumps you into the next tax bracket, you could be giving more in taxes to Uncle Sam than you'd like.

But here's the good news. You may find that negotiating better benefits, rather than a raise, will help you profit more from your good work.

First, you need to know whether your raise is going to put you over the top—into a higher tax bracket. The IRS offers easy-to-use tax bracket tables, which tell what your taxes will be, given your salary. (Just do an online search for "tax brackets," and you'll find dozens of websites with these tables.) Then you can figure out your new taxes and compare them to your raise.

Kyle is just about at his 5-year anniversary with his company—a big deal because the occasion is usually marked with a raise. He's negotiated great benefits packages before, so he knows it's important to be prepared to counter with another option—especially if the raise bumps him into another tax bracket.

Right now, Kyle is earning $33,750 a year. He's heard that he's up for a $6,000 raise, which would bump his salary up to $39,750. This will definitely push him into the next tax bracket. Will he actually see that raise, or will it all go to the IRS?

Kyle hasn't found that right person or had kids, so he's filing as a single taxpayer. Looking at the tax charts, he sees that in this new bracket, his taxes will be $4,750 plus 25% of the amount over $34,500. (That's compared to his current bracket, where he pays $850 plus 15% of the amount over $8,500.) Kyle does the math to find out whether the raise is actually worth it.

To find out how much he currently pays in taxes, he subtracts $8,500 from $33,750, because he pays 15% only on the amount he makes over that.

$$\$33,750 - 8,500 = \$25,250$$

He'll pay 15% of that amount.

$$15\% \text{ of } \$25,250$$
$$0.15 \cdot \$25,250 = \$3,787.50$$

Then he adds the $850 base tax amount.

$$\$3,787.50 + \$850 = \$4,637.50.$$

That's how much Kyle is paying in taxes now. (Of course, various deductions and exemptions might apply, but for purposes of comparison, we just need to know the tax he has to pay before those deductions and exemptions.)

If he gets the raise he thinks he's going to get, he first needs to find the difference between his new salary and $34,500. (The tax schedule says he needs to take 25% of this number.)

$$\$39{,}750 - \$34{,}500 = \$5{,}250$$

That's not what Kyle will pay in taxes. He still needs to take 25% of this figure and then add $4,750 to it.

$$25\% \text{ of } \$5{,}250$$
$$0.25 \cdot \$5{,}250 = \$1{,}312.50$$
$$\$1{,}312.50 + \$4{,}750 = \$6{,}062.50$$

The raise means that he'll be paying a lot more in taxes: $6,062.50 − $4,637.50 = $1,425.

Maybe he's better off asking for another week of vacation, a cappuccino machine in the break room, and a VIP parking space. Kyle gets to work on his counteroffer.

9

In the Gym: How Many Miles on the Treadmill to Burn Off One Doughnut?

You're feeling a little thick around the middle, and your couch is beginning to show signs of permanent stress where you've planted your rear end for the last several months.

It's time to clean out the fridge and hit the gym.

If you've done this before, you know that maintaining weight is a balancing act: Calories in = calories out. To lose weight, you'll need to shake things up:

Fewer calories in + more calories out → weight loss

Yep, there's math involved in losing weight and staying fit. Whether you're at the gym or the kitchen table, a few computations can keep you on the right track.

Your Ideal Weight

There are hundreds of different criteria for tracking changes in your weight—how you look in your favorite pair of jeans, whether you can still play touch football with the guys on the weekends, or whether your snoring is why the next-door neighbor's dog is howling all night long.

But for nutritionists, physicians, and personal trainers, that number on the bathroom scale matters. The pros also count on another important number: BMI, or *body mass index*.

BMI is used to evaluate a person's health on the basis of their body weight and height. Here's the formula:

$$BMI = \frac{703w}{h^2}$$

w is weight in pounds
h is height in inches

Let's say June weighs 155 pounds and is 5 feet 2 inches tall. What is her BMI?

Before you start substituting the numbers into the formula, take a look at what you have. To use the BMI formula, you need to know June's weight (in pounds) and her height (in inches):

w = 155 pounds
h = 5 feet 2 inches

But June's height is listed in feet *and* inches. That number needs to be converted to inches only. There are 12 inches in a foot, so multiply 5 feet by 12 and add the leftover 2 inches, like this:

$(5 \cdot 12) + 2 = 62$ **inches**

Now you can use the BMI formula:

$$BMI = \frac{703w}{h^2}$$

$$BMI = \frac{703 \cdot 155}{62^2}$$

$$BMI = \frac{108,965}{3,844}$$

$$BMI = 28.35$$

June's BMI is 28.35. So what?

We need the experts to tell us what this number means. And they've helpfully provided a chart. (This one comes from the World Health Organization, a group that is usually more concerned with starving children in Africa than with whether you can zip up your pants—but it's still helpful.)

Classification	BMI
Underweight	<18.50
Severe thinness	<16.00
Moderate thinness	16.00–16.99
Mild thinness	17.00–18.49
Normal range	18.50–24.99
Overweight	≥25.00
Pre-obese	25.00–29.99
Obese	≥30.00
Obese class I	30.00–34.99
Obese class II	35.00–39.99
Obese class III	≥40.00

Where does our friend June fit on the BMI table? She's considered overweight and pre-obese. Her doctor should suggest that she lose a few pounds to get into the normal range.

Greater Than, Less Than

What the heck are those funny looking symbols in the BMI table? In case you've forgotten—and don't be embarrassed; it's probably been a while—there's an easy way to remember. The sign opens up in the direction of the larger number.

Symbol	Speak English	Nifty Mnemonic
>	Greater than	BIG number > small number
<	Less than	small number < BIG number

In other words, the big side of the symbol corresponds to the bigger number.

"Greater than or equal to" ($\geq$) and "less than or equal to" ($\leq$) are the hybrids. So if your BMI is 25, are you considered overweight? The table reveals that the answer is yes. That's because when a person's BMI is greater than or equal to 25 (BMI $\geq$ 25), he or she falls in the overweight category.

Now, get on that treadmill.

Eat Less, Move More

Everybody knows someone who can eat anything and stay slim. After devouring her second slice of chocolate-mocha cake with full-fat vanilla ice cream and sprinkles, she leans back in her chair, pats her flat tummy, and says, "I think I may have gained 5 pounds at dinner tonight!"

It's tempting to throw the rest of the cake at her.

It may not be fair, but each of us burns calories differently. Some folks have good genes—they run through calories like water, which means they can eat what they want and forgo long sessions with Claus at the gym. Others seem to gain a pound by simply looking at the leftover French fries on their kid's McDonald's tray.

Fair or not, gender, age, weight, and height all play a role in how efficiently your body handles energy or calories. Did you notice? Many of these variables are numbers. Your age: a number. Your weight: a number. Your height: another number.

And where there are numbers, math is bound to be right around the corner.

Figuring Out Your Basal Metabolic Rate

Your *basal metabolic rate* (BMR) is another important number. It describes how many calories you would need to stay alive if you were to spend all day in bed asleep. In other words, BMR is the minimum calorie intake for a resting individual.

Of course, BMR varies from person to person. If you know your BMR, you can calculate the number of calories you need to consume in a day. But what is BMR based on?

A person's size is important: The more a person weighs, the more energy it takes to do daily tasks. This additional energy translates into a higher BMR. And as we age, we tend to burn calories less efficiently. That's because muscle mass decreases with age—particularly when achy

CHAPTER 9

joints and busy schedules keep us from exercising as frequently. It also means that, in order to maintain your weight as you age, you may need to take in fewer calories—or, better yet, burn more calories.

Finally, because of their muscle mass, men need to consume more calories than women, so gender plays a role. So, there are two formulas for BMR, one for women and one for men.

For Women:

$$655 + (4.3 \bullet \text{weight in pounds}) + (4.7 \bullet \text{height in inches})$$
$$- (4.7 \bullet \text{age in years})$$

For Men:

$$66 + (6.3 \bullet \text{weight in pounds}) + (12.9 \bullet \text{height in inches})$$
$$- (6.8 \bullet \text{age in years})$$

Want to get really geeky? Here are the formulas using variables:

$$BMR_{women} = 655 + 4.3w + 4.7h - 4.7a$$
$$BMR_{men} = 66 + 6.3w + 12.9h - 6.8a$$
$$w \text{ is weight in pounds}$$
$$h \text{ is height in inches}$$
$$a \text{ is age in years}$$

These formulas show that BMR depends on gender, weight, height, and age. In other words, your gender, size, and age play a role in how efficiently you burn calories.

Let's look at an example. Say your best friend, Susan, weighs 185 pounds, is 5 feet 7 inches (67 inches) tall, and is 25 years old. What is her BMR?

To find out, you'll use the formula for women and substitute the information that you have for Susan:

$$655 + (4.3 \bullet \text{weight in pounds}) + (4.7 \bullet \text{height in inches})$$
$$- (4.7 \bullet \text{age in years})$$
$$655 + (4.3 \bullet 185) + (4.7 \bullet 67) - (4.7 \bullet 25)$$
$$655 + 795.5 + 314.9 - 117.5$$
$$1{,}647.9 \text{ calories}$$

Adding in Activity

But remember, BMR tells you how many calories your body will burn if you were asleep all day. And that doesn't require much energy at all. Even climbing out of bed, pouring a cup of coffee, and brushing your teeth burns calories. So to find the number of calories you can burn in a day without gaining weight, you'll need to do one more calculation, and this one is based on your activity level.

$$\text{Total calories} = \text{BMR} + (\text{BMR} \bullet \text{level of activity})$$

Your level of activity is represented as a percent:

- Sedentary $\rightarrow$ 20%
- Lightly active $\rightarrow$ 30%
- Moderately active (exercise most days a week) $\rightarrow$ 40%
- Very active (exercise intensely and daily or for prolonged periods) $\rightarrow$ 50%
- Extra active (hard labor or athletic training) $\rightarrow$ 60%

If you're sedentary, your recommended daily calorie intake would be your BMR plus 20% of your BMR. As an equation, that is

$$\text{Total calories} = \text{BMR} + (\text{BMR} \bullet 0.20)$$

(Did you catch that? You have to turn the percent into a decimal before you can multiply. All you need to do is move the decimal point two places to the left and then drop the percent sign: 20% = 0.20).

Let's take a look at Susan again. Her BMR is 1,647.9. She walks a couple of miles two or three days a week, so she's lightly active. So this is how she'll find the total number of calories she should consume each day to maintain her weight:

$$BMR + (BMR \cdot 0.30)$$
$$1,647.9 + (1,647.9 \cdot 0.30)$$
$$1,647.9 + 494.37$$
$$2,142.27 \text{ calories}$$

(Do you see why she used 0.30, rather than the 0.20 that a sedentary person would use?) In order to maintain her weight, Susan must take in 2,142.27 calories each day.

Fat Chance

A pound of body fat equals just about 3,500 calories. This means that in order to lose 1 pound of fat, you need to consume 3,500 fewer calories (or burn 3,500 *more* calories).

But if you look at those weight-loss advertisements, they make promises like "Lose at least 7 pounds a week on MeltAway, a revolutionary new diet pill that melts fat!" Is that reasonable?

Take a look at the math. To lose 1 pound, you need to reduce your calorie intake by 3,500 (or burn an extra 3,500 calories a day). If you were to lose 7 pounds of fat in a week, you'd be reducing your calorie intake by an average of 3,500 calories every day. Now remember that an average man needs 2,500 calories a day and an average woman needs 2,000. Unless you're consuming an extra 3,500 calories a day, you can't reduce your calories by that much.

Breakfast of Champions

During the 2008 Summer Olympics, swimmer Michael Phelps made big news—not only for his impressive collection of gold medals but also for his eating habits. Rather than the typical 2,500 to 3,000 calories a day that most men need to maintain their weight, Phelps consumed a staggering 12,000 calories each day. The Baltimore Bullet could put away some serious grub.

Here's an example of a Phelps breakfast:

- 3 fried egg sandwiches with cheese, lettuce, tomatoes, fried onions, and mayonnaise
- a 5-egg omelet
- a bowl of grits
- 3 slices of French toast with powdered sugar
- 3 chocolate chip pancakes
- 2 cups of coffee

Most of us would be asleep by 8:30 A.M. on a breakfast like that. What made Phelps different? The number of calories he burned in training each day, of course. If he weren't eating that many calories, he'd lose steam in the middle of his 8-mile-per-day swimming schedule.

But could you burn that many calories a day? Sure, and here's how: 7 hours of high-impact aerobics, 6 hours of mountain biking, 8 hours of golf (carrying your own clubs), or 13 hours of weight lifting. Oh, and those totals? They're daily, not weekly.

So unless those pills are revving up your body, hummingbird-style, if you do lose 7 pounds in a week, it won't be through loss of fat.

Fast and Easy

There simply is no quick or simple way to lose weight, unless you're resorting to unhealthful methods. But there is an easy way to estimate your daily calorie intake. This method isn't as exact as the formula presented earlier, but it works great for those who aren't interested in precision.

To lose fat, eat 12 to 13 calories per pound of bodyweight
To maintain weight, eat 15 to 16 calories per pound of bodyweight
To gain fat, eat 18 to 19 calories per pound of bodyweight

If you weigh 155 pounds, here's your calorie intake for each scenario:

Lose weight → 12 • 155 to 13 • 155—that is,
1,860 to 2,015—calories per day
Maintain weight → 15 • 155 to 16 • 155—that is,
2,325 to 2,480—calories per day
Gain weight → 18 • 155 to 19 • 155—that is,
2,790 to 2,945—calories per day

(Note that these guidelines are the same for men and women. The resulting calories per day might be on the high end for women and on the low end for men.)

Many nutritionists also recommend looking at an average daily calorie intake over a week. If you weigh 155 pounds and average 1,900 calories a day for a week, you're likely to lose weight. If you average 2,800 calories a day for a week, the needle on the scale will probably move up.

A Well-Balanced Nutrition Label

A product's nutrition label is made up of several distinct parts, and each part is designed to help you make good choices about what you're eating. But which numbers are important, and why?

Michael's doctor has warned him, "Watch your fat and sodium intake!" He's also trying to lose a couple of pounds, so it won't hurt to compare nutrition facts. And that's exactly what Michael is doing. He loves soup, and he's trying to decide between two brands.

First, Michael needs to make sure he's comparing tomatoes with tomatoes, so he checks the serving sizes. One serving of Lovely Lentils is 1 cup, and one serving of Barley and Beef is 8 ounces. Are these equivalent? Yes. There are 8 ounces in 1 cup, so Michael (thankfully) doesn't need to do any extra calculations.

Now he needs to consider the fat. What is the percent of calories derived from fat for each soup? To find this, he needs to divide the number of calories from fat by the total number of calories.

$$\text{Lovely Lentils: } 90 \div 210 = 43\%$$
$$\text{Barley and Beef: } 261 \div 320 = 82\%$$

Whoa! Barley and Beef's percent of fat calories is twice as large as that for Lovely Lentils. There's a clear winner here.

Still, Michael wants to look at the amount of sodium in each soup. Again, Lovely Lentils is on top, with a much smaller amount of sodium. And that brand is higher in vitamins A and B, calcium, and iron.

Constant Craving

In many of these formulas, there is something called the *constant*. Just like your mother's *constant* nagging to call home, this is something that never changes.

In the BMI formula, 703 is the constant.

$$BMI = \frac{703w}{h^2}$$

The BMR formulas also have constants, which are shown in bold type here.

$$BMR_{women} = 655 + 4.3w + 4.7h - 4.7a$$
$$BMR_{men} = 66 + 6.3w + 12.9h - 6.8a$$

No matter who uses the formulas, the constants always stay the same.

When *you* use these formulas, you introduce another constant. In the case of the BMI and BMR formulas, your constant is your height. That's a number that probably won't change, although (if you're being honest) your weight and age will.

But there's another reason why Michael should take a closer look at Lovely Lentils: the total calories. If he heats this soup up for lunch, he'll eat fewer calories. Just what the doctor ordered.

The Heart of the Matter

Let's say you want to eat that entire bag of chips at lunch. To balance that out—and not gain weight—you'll have to move your body. There's math involved there, too.

When your heart is working hard, so is your body. So, when you're exercising, you should know how fast your heart is beating. Too close to normal, and you're not exerting enough energy. Too fast, and you could be pushing it.

Your heart rate is measured in beats per minute. Calculating your heart rate is easy: Just find your pulse and count. You could count for an entire minute, but there is an easier way—start at 0 and then count for only 10 seconds. Now you have to do some math.

Let's say that you counted 11 heartbeats in 10 seconds. How many heartbeats would you have in 1 minute? All you need to do is multiply by 6.

$$11 \cdot 6 = 66$$

Why 6? Because there are 60 seconds in a minute, there are six 10-second periods in a minute. (Here's another way to think of it: $60 \div 10 = 6$. And here's another: $10 + 10 + 10 + 10 + 10 + 10 = 60$.) So you need to multiply the number of times your heart beats during each 10-second period (which is 11) by 6.

This result is called your *resting heart rate*, or RHR. Another important number is your *maximum heart rate*, or MHR. This is the fastest your heart should beat, and it is not advisable for it to exceed that rate. You're not necessarily going to keel over if your heart rate reaches its maximum. But you shouldn't exercise for very long when your heart is beating that fast.

There are about half a dozen ways to calculate your maximum heart rate, and all of them come from highly respected experts. But for most folks, a simple formula works just fine:

$$MHR = 220 - age$$

Let's say that you're 40 years old. In that case, your MHR should be $220 - 40 = 180$ beats per minute.

Your RHR and MHR are the bases of the other heart rate zones. And your heart rate zones will help you exercise most efficiently. The American Council on Exercise defines these zones this way:

Intensity of Exercise	Zone
Light to moderate exercise	55–65%
Moderate to vigorous exercise	65–85%
Very vigorous exercise	85%–MHR

Take a look at the table. Should you simply take the percent of your resting heart rate to find how fast your heart should be beating during this kind of exercise? No, because that would put your rate during exercise at *less than* your RHR. That doesn't make sense at all!

In fact, there is a formula you can use to find your target heart rate in each of these zones.

$$(M-R)p=z$$
$$z+R=Z$$

M is maximum heart rate

R is resting heart rate

p is the percent from the Intensity of Exercise table

z is the zone

Z is the zoned heart rate

Let's take a look at an example.

Jesse is a competitive sprinter. In order stay on top of his game, he needs to monitor his heart rate during his daily workout. He's 25 years old, and his RHR is 72 beats per minute (bpm). He has to use a formula to find his MHR:

$$MHR = 220 - age$$
$$MHR = 220 - 25$$
$$MHR = 195 \text{ bpm}$$

Jesse's trainer does the math and comes up with this:

- Jesse's heart rate should not exceed 195 bpm at any time during his workout.
- When he's warming up, his heart rate should be between 140 and 152 bpm.
- When he's in his regular workout period, his rate should be between 152 and 177 bpm.
- And when he does short, intense bursts—such as sprints—his heart rate should be between 177 and 195 bpm.

High-Intensity Interval Training

Mazzy is tired of spending her mornings at the gym. She'd rather be snoozing in bed. Her trainer suggests *high-intensity interval training* (HIIT).

The idea is to switch up the intensity of your exercise—dramatically— which Mazzy's trainer says will make her workout more efficient. The warm-up and cool-down are typical of most exercise routines. But in between, she'll cycle through intense and easy exercise, forcing her heart and muscles to keep up with the sudden changes.

Here's a sample workout:

- Slow walk (warm-up) for 3 minutes
- Fast run for 30 seconds
- Slow walk for 1 minute
- Fast run for 30 seconds
- Repeat previous "walk 1 minute, then run 30 seconds" set for 8 more cycles (9 cycles in all)
- Slow walk (cool down) for 3 minutes

Sounds great, but will Mazzy have time to sleep in and hit the gym before work? Or could she fit it into her lunch hour? Mazzy needs to know how long the workout takes.

$$\text{Warm-up} = 3 \text{ minutes}$$
$$\text{Fast run} = 0.5 \text{ minute}$$
$$\text{Walk/run cycles} = 1.5 \text{ minutes} \cdot 9 \text{ cycles} = 13.5 \text{ minutes}$$
$$\text{Cool-down} = 3 \text{ minutes}$$
$$\text{Total} = 3 + 0.5 + 13.5 + 3 = 20 \text{ minutes}$$

Mazzy can do it! She sets her alarm and hits the pillow happy.

Pumping Iron

Many studies have shown that muscle burns more calories than fat. That idea boils down to an amazing weight-loss secret: If you're more Popeye than Olive Oyl, you may be able to have extra dessert without the extra pounds. That's because adding muscle mass boosts metabolism.

Building muscle offers other health benefits, too. Creaky joints? Muscle strength can help. Worried about osteoporosis? Adding muscle can increase bone density and lower your risk of fractures. Want to reduce your chance of a heart attack? When the body is leaner, your ticker is healthier. (It is a muscle, after all!)

With all of these rewards, who wouldn't want to add strength training to their workout?

Whether you're using free weights or a machine at the gym, there are two parts of strength training: the amount of weight you're lifting and the number of times you repeat each exercise. (Hey! Those are numbers!)

A little bit of math can keep you from being a complete dumbbell at the gym. Take a look at this sample bench-pressing workout.

Bench-Press Workout

	WEEK 1	WEEK 2	WEEK 3	WEEK 4
SET 1	65% • 5	70% • 3	75% • 5	40% • 5
SET 2	75% • 5	80% • 3	85% • 3	50% • 5
SET 3	85% • 5+	90% • 3+	95% • 1+	60% • 5

This chart looks a little like Ahnold's German, so let's break it down. A *set* is the number of times you lift a particular weight in a row. So each time you work out, you'll do three sets. And as the weeks progress, you'll change the number of times you lift that weight.

But how do you know how much weight you should be lifting for each exercise? The chart tells you that, too. But you need some additional information. That's where something called the "1 rep max" comes in.

Also called 1RM, the 1 rep max is the most you can lift in 1 repetition. The percents in the chart refer to the percent of 1RM that you'll lift for each set. So if you can lift 10 pounds as your 1RM, then 85% of that would be 8½ pounds.

As the weeks progress, the sets get more and more intense. You start out lifting 65% of your 1RM, and by the third week, you're lifting 95% of your 1RM. (The last week is a resting week.)

So how do you find your 1RM? You choose a weight to lift for a particular exercise. Do the exercise with that weight. Count how many times you can lift the weight before your muscles are completely fatigued. Then use the Brzycki formula to find your 1RM. Here it is:

$$1RM = w \cdot \frac{36}{37 - r}$$

w is weight

r is the number of repetitions

Let's try it out. Matt can bench-press 100 pounds five times before his muscles are fatigued. What is his 1RM?

$$w = 100$$
$$r = 5$$
$$1RM = 100 \cdot \frac{36}{37 - 5}$$
$$1RM = 100 \cdot \frac{36}{32}$$
$$1RM = 100 \cdot 1.125$$
$$1RM = 112.5$$

So Matt's 1RM is 112.5 pounds.

His personal trainer has suggested that he follow this workout in the first week:

Set 1 → 65% of 1RM, 5 reps
Set 2 → 75% of 1RM, 5 reps
Set 3 → 85% of 1RM, 5 reps

How much will he need to lift for each set?

Set 1 → 65% of 112.5
0.65 • 112.5
73.125
Round to 73 pounds

Set 2 → 75% of 112.5

0.75 • 112.5

84.375

Round to 84 pounds

Set 3 → 85% of 112.5

0.85 • 112.5

95.625

Round to 96 pounds

Once Matt finishes the first month of his workout, he'll need to find his 1RM again. He has gotten stronger, after all! Once he has a new 1RM, he'll adjust his workout, this time adding more weight.

Weighing the Options

Matt has to add weights to the barbell to make it weigh the right amount: 73 pounds, 84 pounds, and so on. But the bar itself weighs something. If he slides 73 pounds of weights onto it, he'll have a barbell that weighs a lot more than 73 pounds. He has to consider how much the bar weighs.

A standard Olympic bar weighs 45 pounds, so how much will Matt need to add to get to 73 pounds?

$$73 - 45 = 28 \text{ pounds}$$

Here's another question to consider: Should Matt add 28 pounds to each side of the bar? Nope. He needs to put half of the 28 pounds on one side of the bar and the other half on the other side.

$$28 \div 2 = 14 \text{ pounds on each side of the bar}$$

The weights Matt is using are available in 50-, 25-, 10-, 5- and 1-pound sizes. What are his options for each side of the bar?

One 10-pound weight and four 1-pound weights

or

Two 5-pound weights and four 1-pound weights

What if Matt doesn't have any 1-pound weights? In that case, he should probably choose one 10-pound weight and one 5-pound weight or three 5-pound weights. How much more will Matt be lifting if he has no 1-pound weights? Just 2 pounds.

10

On the Road: When Will You Get There and How Much Will You Spend?

Sometimes it's just good to get away—to leave the daily grind, stretch out on a beach somewhere, and forget your everyday life.

Just remember, math never takes a holiday.

Whether you're trekking for pleasure or profit, planning your trip will probably require a little addition, subtraction, multiplication and division. But like most everyday math, these calculations don't have to ruin your good time.

Getting There on Time

ETD and ETA—they're such a big deal that everyone knows their acronyms. Your estimated time of departure and estimated time of arrival can make or break a business trip, family vacation, or romantic getaway.

But with time zones and the pesky way that time is measured, figuring out when you'll arrive—or when you'll depart—can be tricky.

Quinton is so ready for spring break. And who wouldn't be happier lying on the beaches of Mexico than trudging the rainy streets of Boston? He's booked the entire week in Cancun and is meeting up with some old friends from high school to boot.

And that's exactly why Leroy left him a message yesterday. Quinton's old buddy is flying in a day earlier than Quinton and has agreed to pick him up from the airport. He just needs to know what time to be there.

The problem is that Quinton doesn't have his airline ticket printed, and he's not near his computer so he can look up the time. He does know these things:

1. He's leaving Boston at 1:30 P.M.
2. He has a 90-minute layover in Chicago.
3. The first leg of his flight is 45 minutes long.
4. The second leg of his flight is 5 hours long.
5. Cancun is 1 hour behind Boston.

Quinton needs to call Leroy back with his arrival time, but first he has to figure out how long he'll be flying and sitting around the Chicago airport—and he also needs to figure in the 1-hour time difference.

He starts by finding the amount of time he'll be flying. For that, he simply needs to add the flight times:

45 minutes + 5 hours = 5 hours and 45 minutes

But he's got that 90-minute layover to consider too, so he adds that.

5 hours and 45 minutes + 90 minutes

Quinton has a few choices now. He could convert everything to minutes and then add. Or he could convert to hours. He thinks a moment before deciding.

If he converts to minutes, he'll have to add some large numbers, and then he'll have to convert back to hours to figure out what time he'll arrive in Mexico. On the other hand, he could convert the minutes to hours and deal with a few fractions instead. Even though fractions look messier, they're sometimes easier to deal with in his head.

Quinton opts for the fractions.

45 minutes is ¾ hour, so

5 hours and 45 minutes is 5¾ hours

and

an additional 90 minutes is 1½ hours

Now the addition is pretty simple:

5¾ + 1½

To handle this without much fanfare, Quinton breaks up the 5¾ into two parts: 5¼ and ½.

5¼ + ½ + 1½

5¼ + 2

7¼

So, Quinton will be traveling for 7 hours and 15 minutes (including his layover). Because he leaves at 1:30 P.M., he'll arrive in Cancun at 8:45 P.M.

Well, not quite. That's still Boston time, so Quinton needs to subtract an hour: otherwise, Leroy will be there an hour behind schedule.

He calls up his good buddy to tell him the news: He'll be there at 7:45 P.M. Just in time for happy hour. (It's always happy hour in Cancun.)

Mixing Things Up

There's no rule in mathematics that says you need to be consistent with the units you use. Every time you solve a problem, you should choose the method that works best for you.

When Quinton was finding the amount of time he was going to be in a plane, he just left his units as hours and minutes. That's because it's pretty simple to add 5 hours to 45 minutes.

But when he got to the next step of his problem—adding the layover—he decided that switching things up a bit would help him out.

When Quinton thought of 5¾ hours as 5½ + ¼ hours, did that make sense to you? If not, try something different. Think of the numbers as decimals. Imagine a clock face. Or get really crazy and picture quarters and dollars. (A quarter is 25¢ or ¼ of a dollar or $0.25.)

Going the Distance

When you're traveling in a different country, you may need to convert metric measures. Here's a quick review:

Metric Conversions

Miles to kilometers	1 mi = 1.61 km	Kilometers to miles	0.621 mi = 1 km
Ounces to grams	1 oz = 28.35 g	Grams to ounces	0.035 oz = 1 g
Pounds to grams	1 lb = 453.59 g	Grams to pounds	0.002 lb = 1 g
Fahrenheit to Celsius	$(F-32) \cdot \dfrac{5}{9}$ or $\dfrac{F-32}{1.8}$	Celsius to Fahrenheit	$\dfrac{9}{5}(C+32)$ or $1.8(C+32)$

Look, your methods don't have to make sense for someone else. They just have to work for you.

Of course, they also need to be mathematically sound, but you might be surprised at how many different ways math can be done—and result in the correct answer.

Over the River and Through the Woods

When you're traveling by car, determining your ETA can be a little tricky. That's because there's no pilot estimating the length of the trip for you.

You'll also need to consider the speed limit, which depends on your route—interstate, curvy country roads, through the city with stop-and-go traffic, or a combination of these. A long stretch of highway isn't the most exciting route to take, but it may be the fastest, simply because you'll probably maintain a steady speed.

These days, your on-board GPS or a good online map can give you the info you need in an instant. But with different state speed limits and routes, you may want to do a little figuring on your own anyway.

Amanda is so exited! Her little sister is having a baby, and she's going to be there for the birth. Mary Helen just called to tell her that she's on her way to the hospital, so Amanda jumps in her car and hits the road.

In preparation for this moment, Amanda did some math last week, to be sure she knew how long it would take her to get there. Mary Helen recently moved to a new city, and Amanda hasn't had a chance to visit yet. She's not worried about getting lost—it's pretty much a straight shot down the interstate—but she is worried about making it there on time.

Using a map, she figures out that it is 180 miles from her house to Mary Helen's hospital. Now all she needs to do is find out how long the drive will take.

She'll be driving from Ohio, where the speed limit is 65 mph, to West Virginia, where it's 70 mph. Nearly all of her driving will be on interstates. How does she come up with her answer?

Amanda could have tallied the number of miles she'd be driving in each state, but when she looked at the map, she noticed that it's just about half-and-half. That level of estimation works for her, so she decides on a plan of action: She'll average the speed limits and then use that result to find how long she'll be driving.

To average two numbers, just add them up and divide by 2. But Amanda's been doing mental math for a long time, and she's got a shortcut for a problem like this one. All she needs to do is find the midpoint of 65 and 70. In other words, she needs to know what number falls exactly between 65 and 70.

Turns out the average is 67.5 mph.

The key in the previous sentence isn't 67.5; it's *mph*, or miles per hour. That's because:

Speed is measured in miles per hour
Speed = miles ÷ hour

To make the math a little easier, let's substitute some variables here (*r* for rate, *d* for distance, and *t* for time).

$$r = \frac{d}{t}$$

First, she substitutes for her variables.

$$67.5 = \frac{180}{t}$$

To get the *t* by itself, she has to multiply each side of the equation by *t*. (Multiplying the right-hand side of the equation by *t* gets rid of it.)

$$67.5t = 180$$

Now she can divide each side of the equation by 67.5 to isolate *t*.

Don't Memorize, Derive

To figure out her trip time, Amanda used some common sense and easy arithmetic. She also derived a very common formula, using an abbreviation she sees every day on her commute: mph.

Yep, Amanda *derived* a formula. That is, she came up with it using information she already knew.

Miles per hour translates to "distance divided by time." And because mph designates the rate (or speed), you can say that *rate is distance divided by time*.

So how do you write that as an equation? Just remember what *is* means, and the rest should be easy.

$$r = \frac{d}{t}$$

Note that *r* is by itself on the left-hand side of the equation. With a teeny-tiny bit of algebra, you can change this equation in a number of different ways, so that you get *d* by itself and then *t* by itself.

$$r = \frac{d}{t}$$

$rt=d$ (Divide each side of the equation by t.)

$t = \dfrac{d}{r}$ (Divide each side of the equation by r.)

You don't have to memorize the equations. In fact, you can derive them with a piece of information from drivers ed: mph is miles per hour.

$$t = \frac{180}{67.5}$$

Finally, she divides 180 by 67.5.

$$t = 2.666 \ldots$$

2.666 . . . is pretty close to 3 hours, and Amanda always needs at least one potty break, so she rounds up.

Unless Mary Helen's labor is really, really short, Amanda should arrive in plenty of time.

Beachin' It

Kathy loves her extended family. She really does. And she really enjoyed their weeklong vacation to the Outer Banks last summer.

Except for one thing: the bickering over money.

A beach vacation isn't cheap, and when you split the costs among four very different-sized families, plus the matriarch, there are bound to be some hard feelings. Something has to be done, or Kathy's not going this year.

She vows to come up with a plan that will make everyone happy.

First, she thinks about where the problems were last year. Her sister Florence, who has 1 child, and her sister Jocelyn, who came by herself, didn't think it was fair that they paid as much as Kathy and their sister Dorothy did. That makes sense, actually, because Kathy has 4 kids and a husband, and Dorothy came with 3 kids and her husband.

Certainly Florence, her daughter, and Jocelyn didn't eat as much as Kathy's family did, and they didn't take up as much room in the house.

Luckily, the house has plenty of space—eight bedrooms that sleep fifteen people in all. And the room assignments worked out pretty well.

Each couple had a room with a double bed, Florence bunked with her daughter, and Jocelyn and Mom each had single rooms. The other seven kids shared the three remaining bedrooms.

Already, Kathy is getting confused, so she decides to make a chart to keep things in order.

SPACE PER FAMILY

Kathy and Ian	Double bed
Dorothy and Charlie	Double bed
Florence and her daughter	Two singles
Jocelyn	Single
Mom	Single
2 kids	Two singles
2 kids	Two singles
3 kids	Two singles and a fold-out bed

Looking at her chart, Kathy has an idea. They're all sharing space, although some families are taking up more room than others. The same goes for groceries. (Kathy figures each family can be responsible for its own entertainment and transportation costs.)

What if she broke up the house and families into shares? The larger families would have larger shares and the smaller families, smaller shares.

Kathy begins by making some assignments. She gives each adult 1 share. All the kids are under 12, so it makes sense to give them a ½ share each.

Another chart arranged by families might help.

CALCULATING SHARES

Kathy and Ian, 4 kids	2 adult shares, 4 kid shares	$2 + 4(\frac{1}{2}) = 2 + 2 = 4$
Dorothy and Charlie, 3 kids	2 adult shares, 3 kid shares	$2 + 3(\frac{1}{2}) = 2 + 1\frac{1}{2} = 3\frac{1}{2}$
Florence, 1 kid	1 adult share, 1 kid share	$1 + \frac{1}{2} = 1\frac{1}{2}$
Jocelyn	1 adult share	1
Mom	1 adult share	1
TOTAL		$4 + 3\frac{1}{2} + 1\frac{1}{2} + 1 + 1 = 11$

So there are a total of 11 shares. Now what?

If the total cost of the beach rental is $3,695, and their groceries last year totaled $1,200, then the entire cost for the week was $4,895. What would happen if Kathy divided that sum by 11? Wouldn't that give her the price per share?

$$4895 \div 11 = 445$$

By Kathy's calculations, each share is worth about $445. Now she needs to find out how much each family owes. Another chart!

SHARES BY FAMILY

Kathy and Ian, 4 shares	$4 \cdot 445 = \$1,780$
Dorothy and Charlie, 3½ shares	$3\frac{1}{2} \cdot 445 = \$1,557.50$
Florence, 1½ share	$1\frac{1}{2} \cdot 445 = \$667.50$
Jocelyn, 1 share	$1 \cdot 445 = \$445$
Mom, 1 share	$1 \cdot 445 = \$445$
TOTAL	$1,780 + 1,557.50 + 667.50 + 445 + 445 = \$4,895$

Looking over her work, Kathy realizes that she could assign the shares very differently. (For example, there could be value in having a "single room," rather than sharing a bedroom.) But this looks like a fair start, anyway.

She crosses her fingers that her brother, sisters, and mom agree.

Processing Process

Kathy really had no idea how to solve her problem at the beginning. There was no formula that she could use or process that she learned from high school. Instead, her plan came from a little bit of brainstorming and a lot of common sense.

For her, creating charts helped organize her information. And she wasn't afraid to try something, such as randomly assigning shares. She also realized that there are probably different ways to solve this problem and that her siblings might not agree with what she came up with.

This is an example of how math can be used to get to an answer, but not necessarily the only answer. It's also an example of how a process develops from exploration.

Math in school is about following a set of steps. Math in everyday life is about taking some chances, seeing what works and what doesn't, and not being afraid to try.

Packaging a Vacation

Going on vacation means packing, finding someone to take care of Fido, and taking some time off from work. It also means charging some pretty hefty items on your credit card.

The finances of vacationing can boggle the mind. And even with online trip planners and the ability to comparison-shop with the click of a mouse, planning a vacation can make you ready for *another* vacation.

Red and Emily are ready for their second honeymoon. After 25 years of marriage, two kids, and the stress of everyday life, they deserve it. So Red is going to surprise Emily on their anniversary with a 1-week getaway to Aruba.

For 5 years, he's been secretly putting away a little cash here and there. He's got $7,500 saved up, and that's just enough to whisk his bride away for some R & R. (That's romance and rest.) Red has even arranged for Emily to take some time off from work.

But first he's got to figure out how he can spend his vacation nest egg. After Emily goes to sleep, he cruises trip-planning websites looking for the best deal. And he's very quickly overwhelmed.

There are all-inclusive packages, non-inclusive packages, romance packages, and adventure packages. Some include the cost of flights and drinks and meals. Others offer some combination of these features.

It's going to be a long night.

Within an hour or so, Red has some options scribbled down on a piece of paper. He has chosen their destination—a secluded resort with 5-star dining, access to a private beach, a spa, and great online reviews. Now it's on to the pricing. There are a number of options:

- All-inclusive, including travel: $7,225
- Romance package (all-inclusive, without travel, and including a champagne breakfast and moonlight cruise): $6,150
- Hotel + Travel package, without activities, meals, and drinks: $4,140
- Everything à la carte: $3,450

Because two of his options don't include airfare, Red prices out some flights. He finds out that he can get two round-trip tickets for about $925. Not bad!

If he chooses a non-inclusive option, he'll need to pay for meals, drinks, and activities. And that requires more research. Red wonders whether there is a good way to estimate these.

He considers meals first. The resort includes a free breakfast, so he won't need to include that in his calculations. But unless they're going with the all-inclusive option, they will have to buy lunches and dinners. Red does some more research and comes up with the following numbers:

Average lunch → $25/person
Average dinner → $60/person

And because there are two of them, and they'll be there for 7 full days:

Lunches: $50 per day for 7 days = $350
Dinners: $120 per day for 7 days = $840

It looks like the cost of meals will be $350 + $850, or $1,190.

He and Emily aren't big drinkers, so that's pretty simple to figure out. Assuming that the cost of drinks is pretty high, he guesses $25 a day for two fancy cocktails, and if they have a nice bottle of wine with dinner each night, that'll run them about $200 for the week.

$$(\$25 \cdot 7) + \$200 = \$375$$

Now, Red thinks about activities. A day on a sailboat and some snorkeling sounds great ($450). Then he'd like to book a few spa treatments for Emily ($500).

$$\$450 + \$500 = \$950$$

Because all of the prices so far have included tax, Red doesn't need to do any math for that. But he will need to tip the baggage carriers, taxi drivers, servers, and spa staff. Red takes a shot in the dark, and guesses

$350 for all gratuities. (That could be too much, but it's probably not going to be too little.)

This is a ton of information, and Red's legal pad looks like a football coach's playbook. He'd better get organized if he wants to book this trip and get some sleep. Red decides to make a list.

PACKAGE	EXTRAS	TOTAL
All-inclusive: $7,225	none	$7,225
Romance package: $6,150	$925 (air)	$7,075
Hotel + Travel: $4,140	$1,915 (meals, etc.) + $950 (activities)	$7,005
A la carte: $3,450	$925 (air) + $1,915 (meals, etc.) + $950 (activities)	$7,240

Now Red can really consider his options.

The most expensive choice is à la carte, but all of the totals are pretty darned close. If he goes by price alone, the clear winner is the Hotel + Travel package. But that requires him to handle everything on his own—and honestly, he's ready for bed.

On the other hand, the Romance package is only $70 more. And right now, that extra bit of cash seems worth it. Red pulls out his credit card and books their flights and vacation packages. Then he snuggles up next to Emily and savors his little surprise!

Taking a Chance in Vegas

There's probably no other destination in the world more math-centric than Vegas. Between the gambling and 2-for-1 prime rib dinners, math problems abound.

A Little Somethin' Somethin'

No matter where you are in the world, you are expected to tip. And that little bit of math is not exactly what you want to be doing when you're relaxing.

Never fear! There is a simple way to figure out the tip on any bill—whether it's for drinks, a meal, a taxi, or even the tour guide.

First, round your total. There's no reason to kill any brain cells figuring the tip on $37.99, when $38 is so close.

(And here's another tip: Unless the total change is less than a dime, round up. That little extra probably isn't going to make you broke.)

If you've had really good service, 20% of the bill is standard. To find it, just divide the total by 5. (That's because 20% is the same thing as $\frac{1}{5}$.) Suppose your bill is for $45.60. Round up to $46. Then

$$46 \div 5 = 9\tfrac{1}{5} \text{ or } \$9.20$$

Or you can find 10% of the total and double it.

$$10\% \text{ of } 46 \text{ is } \$4.60$$
$$2 \cdot \$4.60 = \$9.20$$

Finding 15% is a little trickier, but it can be done mentally in three little steps. Just find 10% of the total. Then halve the total (that's 5%). Then add these two results.

$$10\% \text{ of } 46 \text{ is } \$4.60$$
$$\$4.60 \div 2 = \$2.30$$
$$\$4.60 + \$2.30 = \$6.90$$

Winning isn't everything, but too many Vegas vacationers incorrectly assume that they can come home with more money than they brought. These high hopes translate into high energy.

It's not until you leave that you notice the big rip-off.

But why is it so hard to win at gambling? The answer is simple: The odds of your winning are very, very low. Of course, the actual odds depend on the game itself. You can lose your shirt in an hour's time playing slots, but with a little strategy, you *might* come out on top at the craps table.

Still, these games are designed to favor the casino itself. (They are profit-seeking ventures, after all.) And so gamblers are well advised to keep an eye on their bets.

Despite all of these truths, Zoe is absolutely thrilled to go to Las Vegas with her girlfriends. And this story gets even better—she won the trip in a random drawing at her local hard-rock radio station. With this winning streak, she's sure to hit the jackpot!

She doesn't want to think too much, and she finds slots incredibly boring, so Zoe decides that roulette is her game. As soon as she unpacks in the casino's hotel, she heads down to the roulette wheel to get her bearings.

Odds of Winning

Roulette is a very simple game, it turns out. The object is to predict where the ball will land on the wheel. Each of the 38 slots is numbered (0, 00, and 1–36) and is either red or black (except for the 00 and 0 slots, which are green). Zoe watches the game for a while, looking for patterns and possible strategies.

Pretty quickly, she notices that there are several different ways to place a bet. She wonders if there is a list in her Vegas guidebook, so she pulls it out of her back pocket to check. Sure enough, there is:

Inside Bets		Outside Bets	
Straight up	Single number	*Red*	Red number
Split	One of two numbers	*Black*	Black number
Street or *Line*	One of three numbers	*Odd*	Odd number
Corner or *Quad*	One of four numbers	*Even*	Even number
Basket	One of: 00, 0, 1, 2, 3	*Dozens*	One of 12 consecutive numbers
Double street	One of six numbers	*Column*	One of 12 numbers in a column

As she's watching, Zoe notices something else—it's very difficult to win at roulette. For one thing, each time the ball is dropped, the chances are the same. In other words, it doesn't matter how long she plays, she'll have exactly the same chance of winning on every single bet.

Second, the odds of each win are pretty small. Take the straight-up bet, for example. There are 38 possible outcomes: the numbers 1–36, along with 0 and 00. (You can't bet on 0 or 00 on a straight-up bet.) Zoe is betting on only one of those outcomes. So the odds of her winning are 1:38. The odds of winning any of the other bets are also low, although calculating those odds is more complicated. What if Zoe put down an outside red bet? What would be her chances of winning?

Two of the roulette slots are green, so that means 36 of them are red or black. Half of those 36 are actually red, so Zoe has 18 chances to win. The odds of her winning are 18 out of 38. Hmm, that doesn't look so bad, does it?

$$18:38 \text{ or } \frac{18}{38}$$

If she changed the fraction to a percent (that is, if she divided 18 by 38), she'd find out that her chance is 47%. That's less than her chances of getting heads when she flips a coin.

Zoe's enthusiasm is dropping like a stone. This gambling thing is looking less and less like a sure thing.

Just to be sure, Zoe considers one more bet: the basket. If she bets that 00, 0, 1, 2, or 3 will come up, how are her chances? Turns out, not so good. She wants 1 of 5 possibilities, but there are 38 possibilities in all:

$$\frac{5}{38}$$

Estimating, she sees that her chances of winning are between 1:7 and 1:8, or between 13% and 14%.

Why does she do this instead of finding out what 5 ÷ 38 is?

First, she notices that $\frac{5}{38}$ does not reduce easily. But she also notices that 38 is between 35 and 40, which are multiples of 5. And she knows that $\frac{5}{35}$ reduces to $\frac{1}{7}$ and that $\frac{5}{40}$ reduces to $\frac{1}{8}$.

Make sense? Good.

Now, Zoe happens to know that $\frac{1}{7}$ is about 14%. You may not have that little bit of information in your mental reserve. But you may know that $\frac{1}{8} = 0.125$, or 12.5%. And you probably know that $\frac{1}{7}$ is a little bit bigger than $\frac{1}{8}$.

So you can check Zoe's mental math—the odds of a basket bet are a bit higher than 13%.

Zoe's too cautious to play such terrible odds. But maybe another game is a better choice? She strolls over to the craps table to see.

House Rules

The payout for casino gambling is the amount paid on each winning bet. So if the payout is 15:1, you get 15 times the bet you placed, plus the amount you bet. Here's an example:

Original bet → $4
Payout → 15:1
Amount won → (4 • $15) + $15 = $75

You'd think these payouts are related to the odds—and they are, but not exactly. For example, the payout on roulette is expressed by this formula:

$$payout = \frac{36 - n}{n}$$

n is the number of chances to win

So, if you made an outside black bet, you'd have 18 chances to win. That means your payout would be

$$\frac{36 - 18}{18} = \frac{18}{18} \text{ or } 1:1$$

In this case, you'd get back the amount you bet, plus your bet.

Appendix

Fabulous Formulas

Amount-Due Formula (Chapter 2)

$$A = P(1+r)^n$$

where A is amount due on the loan, P is the principal, r is the compound interest rate, and n is the number of compounding periods in the loan

Area (Chapters 4 and 6)

AREA OF A SQUARE

$A = s^2$, where s is the length of a side

AREA OF A RECTANGLE

$A = l \cdot w$, where l is length and w is width

AREA OF A TRIANGLE

$A = \frac{1}{2}hb$, where h is the height of the triangle and b is the base

AREA OF A CIRCLE

$A = \pi r^2$, where π is 3.14 . . . and r is the radius

Basal Metabolic Rate, or BMR (Chapter 9)

$$\text{BMR}_{\text{women}} = 655 + 4.3w + 4.7h - 4.7a$$
$$\text{BMR}_{\text{men}} = 66 + 6.3w + 12.9h - 6.8a$$

where w is weight, h is height, and a is age

Body Mass Index, or BMI (Chapter 9)

$$BMI = \frac{703w}{h^2}$$ where w is weight and h is height

Brzycki Formula (Chapter 9)

$$1RM = w \cdot \frac{36}{37 - r}$$

where 1RM is the 1-repetition maximum, w is the weight used, and r is the number of repetitions

Debt-to-Income Ratio (Chapter 8)

$$\frac{debt}{income}$$

Monthly Payment Formula (Chapters 2 and 8)

$$M = \frac{P\left(\dfrac{r}{12}\right)}{1 - \left(1 + \dfrac{r}{12}\right)^{-n}}$$

where M is the monthly payment, P is the principal (or the amount borrowed), r is the monthly interest rate, and n is the number of months in the loan

Monthly Lease Payment (Chapter 2)

Monthly lease payment = depreciation fee + finance fee + sales tax
Depreciation fee = (cap cost − residual value) ÷ lease term
Finance fee = (cap cost − residual value) • money factor
Sales tax = monthly payment • sales tax rate

where the *cap cost* is the amount financed (the cost of the vehicle, plus any dealers costs) and the *money factor* is the interest rate

Maximum Heart Rate, or MHR (Chapter 9)

$MHR = 220 - a$, where a is age

Net Worth Formula (Chapter 8)

Net worth = assets − liabilities

Principal Formula (Chapter 3)

$$P = M\left(\frac{(1+r)^n - 1}{r(1+r)^n}\right)$$

where P is principal, M is the monthly payment, r is the monthly interest rate, and n is the number of months in the loan.

Rule of 72 (Chapter 8)

$y = 72 \div r$, where y is years and r is rate

Simple Interest Formula (Chapter 8)

$I = Prt$
where I is the interest, P is the principal, r is the rate, and t is the length of the loan.

Target Heart Rate (Chapter 9)

$z = p(M - R)$

$Z = z + R$

where M is maximum heart rate, R is resting heart rate, p is the percent from the heart-rate-zones table, z is the zone, and Z is the zoned heart rate

Total-Payment Formula (Chapter 3)

$T = M \bullet n$

where T is the total payment, M is the monthly payment, and n is total number of months in the loan

Surface Area (Chapter 4)

In general, the surface area of an object is the sum of the areas of its faces or sides.

SURFACE AREA OF A CUBE

$SA = 6s^2$, where SA is surface area and s is the length of each edge of the cube.

SURFACE AREA OF A RECTANGULAR PRISM

$SA = 2lw + 2lh + 2wh$, where SA is surface area, l is length, w is width, and h is height

SURFACE AREA OF A CYLINDER

$SA = 2\pi r^2 = 2\pi rh$, where SA is surface area, π is 3.14 . . . , r is the radius of the base, and h is the height of the cylinder

SURFACE AREA OF A SPHERE

$SA = 4\pi r^2$, where SA is surface area, π is 3.14 . . . , and r is the radius of the sphere

Volume (Chapter 6)

VOLUME OF A CUBE

$V = s^3$, where s is the length of a side

VOLUME OF A RECTANGULAR PRISM

$V = lwh$, where l is the length, w is the width, and h is the height

VOLUME OF A CYLINDER

$V = \pi r^2 h$, where π is 3.14 ... , r is the radius of the base, and h is the height of the cylinder

VOLUME OF A PYRAMID

$V = \frac{1}{3}(lwh)$, where l is the length, w is the width, and h is the height

VOLUME OF A CONE

$V = \frac{1}{3}(\pi r^2 h)$

Glossary

Consider this glossary a tool in your mathematical tool belt. If you need to double-check a definition (say, for instance, you want to review what an improper fraction is), you can find the answer here. In some cases, we have included definitions that are related to concepts we discussed, even if the word or phrase itself wasn't used in this book.

This list is reserved for math terms, so you won't find definitions for *principal* or *compound interest* here. For that, take a look at the Index, and it will direct you to the pages where the concepts are discussed.

So go ahead. Dig into some meaty math definitions. Soon you'll be able to impress the kids and be the geeky star at your next cocktail party.

Additive Identity

Adding zero to a number leaves it unchanged. $x+0=x$. Example: $3+0=3$

Additive Inverse

The number you add to another number to get zero; the negative value of a positive number and the positive value of a negative number. Example: The additive inverse of 12 is -12, because $12+(-12)=0$. And the additive inverse of -1 is 1, because $-1+1=0$.

Algebra

The field of mathematics in which letters and other symbols are used to represent numbers.

Algorithm

A set of steps used to solve a problem.

Angle

A two-dimensional figure formed by two rays that share a common endpoint called the *vertex*.

Area

The amount of space occupied by a two-dimensional figure. Area is expressed in squared units.

Arithmetic

Basic operations (addition, subtraction, multiplication, and division) with whole numbers, fractions, decimals, and exponents.

Base-10 Number System

The decimal system of numbers, which has 10 as its operating base.

Circumference

The distance around a circle or other closed curve.

Coefficient

A number that is multiplied by a variable. Example: In $5x$, 5 is the coefficient.

Common Denominator

The same denominator in two or more fractions.

Commutative Property of Addition and Multiplication

$a+b=b+a$ and $a \bullet b = b \bullet a$. Addition and multiplication are commutative because you can change the order of the numbers and still get the same answer. Examples: $2+1=1+2=3$ and $4 \bullet 9 = 9 \bullet 4 = 36$.

Constant

A fixed value. Example: 10 is a constant in the expression $6x^2 + 10$.

Decimal Number

A number that includes a decimal point followed by digits. The digits to the right of the decimal point indicate values smaller than 1. Example: 5.7903

Denominator

The bottom number in a fraction. Example: The denominator of $\frac{1}{5}$ is 5.

Dependent Variables

Variables whose values are determined by the values of another variable (usually the *independent variable*). Example: In finding the cooking time of a turkey, the time you seek is the dependent variable, because it depends on the weight of the bird (which is the independent variable).

Difference

The answer in a subtraction problem. Example: The difference of 5 and 2 is 3.

Digit

A symbol used to make numerals. Example: 1, 4, and 7 are digits of 147.

Distributive Property of Multiplication over Addition

$a(b+c)=ab+ac$. When a number is multiplied by the sum of two other numbers, the first number can be distributed to both of those numbers (that is, multiplied by each of those numbers independently) and the results then added. Examples: $5(2+4)=10+20=30$ and $3(x+2)=3x+6$.

Dividend

In a division problem, the amount being divided into parts. Example: In the problem, $20 \div 5 = 4$, 20 is the dividend.

Divisor

In a division problem, the number that is being divided into another number (called the *dividend*). Example: In the problem $20 \div 5 = 4$, 5 is the divisor.

Equation

A mathematical sentence that states equality. Examples: $4+2=6$ and $7x-9=27$

Estimation

An educated guess, usually based on rounding the numbers before using any operations. An estimate is not an exact answer. Example: An estimate for $19 \bullet 4$ is 80.

Exponent

The exponent of a number tells how many times the number is to be multiplied by itself. Example: In x^5, 5 is the exponent, and $x^5 = x \bullet x \bullet x \bullet x \bullet x$.

Expression

Numbers, symbols, and operations grouped together.

Example: $6x+9$

Factor

The numbers you multiply together to get another number. Also, a number that will divide evenly into another number. Example: 2 is a factor of any even number.

Fraction

Part of a whole, written $\frac{a}{b}$, where a is any whole number, and b is any whole number. Examples: $\frac{2}{3}$ and $\frac{9}{4}$

Greatest Common Factor (GCF)

The largest number that will divide evenly into two or more numbers. Example: 12 is the GCF of 60 and 24.

Improper Fraction

A fraction whose numerator is larger than its denominator. An improper fraction is always larger than 1. Improper fractions can be written as *mixed numbers*. Example: $\frac{10}{3}$

Independent Variable

A variable whose value determines the value of other variables. Example: In finding the cooking time of a turkey, the weight of the bird is the independent variable, because it determines the cooking time (which is the *dependent variable*).

Integer

A number with no fractional part. The set of integers is $\{\ldots, -4, -3, -2, -1, 0, 1, 2, 3, 4, \ldots\}$.

Inverse

The opposite. Examples: The inverse of multiplying by 2 is dividing by 2. The inverse of adding 7 is subtracting 7. The inverse of $\frac{2}{3}$ is $\frac{3}{2}$.

Least Common Denominator (LCD)

In a series of fractions, the smallest number that all of the denominators will divide into evenly. Example: 8 is the least common denominator for $\frac{1}{2}$, $\frac{1}{2}$, and $\frac{1}{8}$.

Least Common Multiple (LCM)

The smallest number that is a common multiple of two or more numbers. Example: The LCM for 3 and 6 is 12.

Mixed Number

A number that includes a whole number and a fraction. Mixed numbers can be written as improper fractions. Example: 4¾

Multiplication Property of Equality

When both sides of an equation are multiplied by the same number, the equation stays true. If $a = b$, then $ac = bc$.

Multiple

The product of two numbers; also, a number that can be divided evenly by another number. Example: 25 is a multiple of 5.

Multiplicative Identity

Multiplying a number by 1 equals that number. Examples: $4 \cdot 1 = 4$ and $a \cdot 1 = a$.

Number Sense

The ability to use and understand numbers. Number sense includes an understanding of number values, operations (including their properties), and estimation.

Numerator

The top number of a fraction. Example: 6 is the numerator of $\frac{6}{7}$.

Operation

A mathematical calculation, most commonly addition, subtraction, multiplication, and division.

Order of Operations

The order in which calculations must be performed in an expression: parentheses, exponents, multiplication, division, addition, and subtraction.

PEMDAS

A way of remembering the order of operations: Parentheses, Exponents, Multiplication, Division, Addition, and Subtraction. PEMDAS comes from this mnemonic: Please Excuse My Dear Aunt Sally.

Percent

One part of 100 represented with a percent sign (%). Example: More than 25% of the cars were red.

Percentage

A portion of the whole, usually stated in a general sense. Example: The percentage of red cars on the road has increased significantly over the last year.

Perimeter

The distance around a two-dimensional shape. The perimeter of a circle is called the circumference.

Probability

The chance that something will (or will not) happen.

Product

The answer in a multiplication problem. Example: The product of 2 and 5 is 10.

Quotient

The answer in a division problem. Example: In the problem $20 \div 5 = 4$, 4 is the quotient.

Ratio

A comparison of two numbers. Ratios can be written with a colon, a fraction line or the word *to*. Examples: 2:1, $\frac{2}{1}$, and 2 to 1.

Recurring Decimal

A decimal number whose digits behind the decimal point infinitely repeat. Recurring decimals are always rational numbers. Examples: 0.333 . . . and 0.2388. . . . Recurring decimals are often shown with a bar over the recurring digit or digits. The bar indicates which digits repeat. Examples: $2.\overline{3}$ and $17.\overline{78}$

Reflexive Property of Equality

Any number is equal to itself. $a = a$. Example: $3 = 3$

Remainder

The amount left over after division. Example: $15 \div 4 = 3$ with a remainder of 3. If a divisor is a factor of the dividend, the remainder is 0.

Rounding

Reducing the number of digits in a number (or making them 0) but keeping the value of the rounded number close to the value of the original number. Numbers can be rounded to a variety of places, including the ones place, 10ths, 1000ths, etc. Examples: $3.56 \rightarrow 3.6$ and $7.13 \rightarrow 7$

Sequence

A list of objects or numbers in a special order. Example: 6, 12, 24, 48, . . . is a geometric sequence.

Side

One of the line segments that defines a two-dimensional shape, or one of the surfaces that defines a three-dimensional shape.

Simplify

In mathematics, this means to put in the simplest form.

Example: Simplify the fraction $\dfrac{5}{10}$. (Answer: ½) Example: Simplify the algebraic expression $2(x+7)$ (Answer: $2x+14$)

Square

Multiplying a number by itself. Example: $4^2 = 4 \bullet 4 = 16$

Sum

The answer in an addition problem. Example: The sum of 4 and 7 is 11.

Surface Area

The total area of a three-dimensional figure, such as a cube, cylinder, or prism.

Symmetric Property of Equality

If $a = b$, then $b = a$. Example: If $x = 3$, then $3 = x$.

Term

Part of an algebraic expression that includes a number, a variable, or the product of numbers and variables. Terms are separated by addition or subtraction symbols. Example: The terms of $6x^2 + 4x - 2$ are $6x^2$, $4x$, and 2.

Transitive Property of Equality

If $a = b$ and $b = c$, then $a = c$. Example: If $x = y$ and $y = 2$, then $x = 2$.

Variable

A symbol for an unknown number. A variable is usually a letter. Example: The variable in $2x + 9$ is x.

Vertex

A point where two or more line segments meet. The plural of vertex is vertices. Angles, squares, triangles, rectangles, cubes, prisms, and pyramids have vertices.

Volume

The amount of three-dimensional space an object occupies. Volume is expressed in cubic units.

Whole Number

A positive number with no fractional or decimal parts. The set of whole numbers is {0, 1, 2, 3, 4, . . . }. Examples: 4, 17, and 399

Index

A

Addition
  doing same thing to both sides of
    equation, 41
  estimating answers. *See* Estimating
  of fractions, 113–14, 115–16, 144
  inverse of, 44
  of negative numbers, 7
  order of operations (PEMDAS
    acronym), 36
  rounding before, 3
  of time, 108–9
  word clues indicating, 134
Amount-due formula $(A = P(1 + r)^n)$,
  35–37
Appliance (refrigerator)
  measurements, 87–88
Area calculations
  carpet requirements, 83–85
  circles, 221
  formulas, 81, 221
  oddly shaped areas, 123–25
  paint requirements, 78–82
  perimeter calculations, 123

rectangles, 221
scale drawings and, 86
square feet, 78–80, 84, 125
squares, 221
square yards, 84
subscripts in, 85
surface area, 81, 129, 135–36, 224
triangles, 221
windows, doors and, 79–82
Art, hanging, 88–92

B

Basal metabolic rate (BMR), 185–88,
  192, 222
Birdhouse calculations, 153–54
Body mass index (BMI), 182–84, 192,
  222
Bottled water vs. filtered water costs,
  21
Brzycki formula, 198, 222
Budget. *See also* Debt; Retirement
  adjusting spending based on, 159
  average percents of select expenses,
    158

About the Author

When people learn that Laura Laing has a degree in mathematics, it's always the same reaction: Widening eyes change to a puzzled look and then, "But aren't you a writer?" Laura contends that writing great nonfiction is not much different from proving $a(b+c)=ab+ac$, except she gets to use words that are a whole lot more fun.

After receiving her undergraduate degree from James Madison University, Laura taught high school math for four years in a rural town in eastern Virginia. She left the classroom in favor of marketing, public relations, volunteer coordination, and development.

She then made the transition to journalism, working as a content producer/editor for the country's first online version of a regional, daily newspaper and then as a reporter for the regional, weekly business publication *Inside Business* in Norfolk, Virginia.

As a freelance writer, she has written for regional and national publications, including *Parade, Parents, Pregnancy*, and Southwest Airline's *Spirit* magazine. Her career has now come full circle, as she has taken on more and more curriculum development projects. She has served as the instructional designer for Algebra II and Probability and Statistics courses, as well as writing mathematics test items for state standardized tests.

Born in Tuscon, Arizona and having spent most of her life in Virginia, she now calls Baltimore, Maryland home.